JESSE'S BOOK OF
CREOLE AND DEEP SOUTH
RECIPES

JESSE'S BOOK

OF

CREOLE

AND

DEEP SOUTH
RECIPES

By Edith Ballard Watts

with John Watts

WEATHERVANE BOOKS
NEW YORK

CONTENTS

FOREWORD

Jesse came to our family in Bay St. Louis, Mississippi, thirty-eight years ago, a gangling Negro boy of fifteen with a pleasant disposition, a happy imagination, and a capacity for work. He already knew how to cook simple Southern dishes, an art he had picked up on crew boats around Mississippi Sound and in various kitchens of summer resorters who made the Gulf Coast their home and playground from May until October.

Mother took him in hand and taught him how to prepare and serve properly and smoothly the famous Creole dishes of New Orleans, and adapt the exotic and flavorsome meat, game, and fowl concoctions of the Deep South to the fastidious taste of Father and his gourmet friends, and to the exigencies of our growing family.

During the next twenty-five years, while Jesse ruled our kitchen, the Ballard dining table became the Mecca of noted men and women in the fields of education, music, medicine, politics, publishing, religion, and government—a place where fine food vied with sparkling conversation.

Men like Henry L. Mencken, Paul de Kruif, and Henry Luce exclaimed over Jesse's Diamond-Back Terrapin, while archbishops and other princes of the church smacked their lips over Jesse's Redfish Creole, Wine-Merchant Sauce, Oyster Cutlets, and Shrimp Jambalaya. Dorothy Dix, who lived "across the bay," admired Jesse's Red Snapper Court Bouillon particularly, and Richard Bonelli, the Metropolitan Opera star, one memorable Sunday burst into song as a tribute to his introduction to a real Louisiana Creole Gumbo cooked by Jesse's sure hand.

Those were golden days indeed. They are gone now, but Jesse is still with us, still simple, affable, and always courteous, and still the undisputed factotum of the family's separate, scattered kitchens whenever any one of the five children that Jesse helped to raise wants to put on the dog in a culinary way on some special occasion.

We hope you like these recipes and the results you will obtain if you follow Jesse's suggestions and instructions closely. They have stood the test of time, and they are authentic Creole and Deep South cookery. The Key West recipes come from my husband's side of the family, and they are unusual too.

EDITH BALLARD WATTS

Gulfport, Mississippi

JESSE'S BOOK OF
CREOLE AND DEEP SOUTH
RECIPES

❦ 1 ❦

APPETIZERS

A Showy Shrimp Buffet

This dish is sure to cause oh's and ah's even before it is tasted. However, like all of Jesse's favorite recipes, this one doesn't rely merely on its immense eye appeal, as "fancy" dishes often do; it tastes even better than it looks. But don't think you can just boil the shrimp in plain salted water. To be sure, the looks of the dish may be the same, but the flavor won't keep the guests exclaiming as it will if you boil the shrimp exactly as Jesse does. Do not shell the shrimp until the day you are to serve them. They will keep very well overnight after boiling, but they lose juice and flavor if the shells are removed. Serves 6 to 8.

FOR BOILING THE SHRIMP

3 to 4 tablespoons salt

15 to 20 whole allspice

6 or 8 whole black peppercorns and a generous sprinkling of ground black pepper

3 or 4 dashes cayenne pepper or Tabasco Sauce

juice and rind of ½ lemon

15 to 20 whole cloves

6 cloves garlic, sliced

3 small or 2 large onions, sliced

2 large stalks fresh celery, crushed or broken

2 large bay leaves

2 pinches dried or 1 sprig fresh thyme

several sprigs fresh parsley

few bits of dried red pepper (don't go too heavy here)

1 tablespoon Worcestershire sauce

2½ to 3 lbs. medium to large fresh or frozen headless shrimp (if they are not headless, add an extra ½ lb.)

Season 2 to 2½ quarts water with a heaping tablespoon of salt to each quart of water, and add salt until the water is slightly saltier than that you would ordinarily use for cooking vegetables. Add the next thirteen ingredients to the water and bring to a boil and let simmer for at least 20 minutes before adding the shrimp. After adding the shrimp, watch the pot until the water comes back to a boil, and cook the shrimp 12 to 15 minutes, according to their size—small to medium-sized ones cook in less time than very large ones. The more uniform in size the shrimp are, the better your dish will look, since overcooked shrimp do not shell so easily or remain so shiny and firm as ones that are not overdone. Also, in order to prevent shrimp from getting soggy or broken, do not allow them to stand in water but remove them from the fire and drain them in a colander for cooling.

FOR COMPLETING THE BUFFET

1 *large head white cabbage*
1 *wedge imported Roquefort cheese*
1 *glass Roquefort cheese spread*
¾ *teaspoon cream-style horseradish*

2 *or 3 dashes Tabasco Sauce*
1½ *tablespoons scraped onion*
3 *to 4 tablespoons mayonnaise*
1 *can or jar pitted large black olives*
potato chips

To prepare the buffet, secure a large, symmetrically shaped, firm head of white cabbage and remove outer leaves carefully so that the delicate light-green foliage is left smooth and lovely to look at. This is to be the base of your shrimp buffet. Turn the cabbage head upside down, and shave a bit from its top, if necessary, to make the head sit perfectly steadily on a platter. With a sharp paring knife, cut out the cabbage stalk and scoop a deep hole by scraping and slivering out the cabbage around the stalk space. Thus you have a bowl made from the head of cabbage, and into this cabbage cup you can place the shrimp sauce at the last minute before serving.

ROQUEFORT SHRIMP SAUCE

To make the shrimp sauce, crush and blend a small section of imported Roquefort cheese into a glassful of Roquefort cheese spread until the mixture is smooth and without lumps—a fork works best for this. Add the horseradish, Tabasco, and onion. (Jesse usually takes a very small white onion and scrapes it into the dressing with a sharp knife, scraping from each side until the juice and pulp seem gone. Careful here. Too much onion ruins the result.) Thin the mixture with 3 to 4 tablespoons mayonnaise (not salad dressing) until it is pliable enough to allow easy dipping of the shrimp. Because that's what your guests will do— dip their shrimp into the delectable concoction as they "pick" them from the cabbage bowl.

To complete the buffet, shell the shrimp and pin them all over the cabbage "bowl" with white toothpicks, and between the shrimp pin on the shiny black olives. The more shrimp and olives you get on, the better the finished product will look. Fill the cabbage hollow with sauce, and pile a ring of fluffy, golden, crisp potato chips around the cabbage. When the shrimp run out, your guests will just as delightedly dip up whatever sauce is left with the potato chips. (You can very easily use the cabbage for dinner next day—if one of the guests doesn't snitch it, as on one occasion one of our own guests actually did!)

SPECIAL SHRIMP COCKTAIL SAUCE

1 *cup chili sauce*
⅛ *teaspoon garlic salt or 1 small garlic clove put through garlic press*
2 *tablespoons Worcestershire sauce*
juice of ½ lemon
¼ *teaspoon Creole mustard*
2 *teaspoons finely chopped celery (preferably put through garlic press)*
½ *teaspoon grated onion*

Mix all ingredients together. Serves 6 to 8.

Shrimp Remoulade

½ cup mayonnaise
½ cup Creole mustard
½ clove garlic put through garlic press, or ⅛ teaspoon garlic salt
½ medium-sized onion
salt and pepper to taste

1 teaspoon very finely chopped celery (preferably put through garlic press)
2 teaspoons Worcestershire sauce
1 tablespoon lemon juice
⅛ teaspoon sugar

Mix all ingredients together, scraping the onion into the sauce. This is usually served over shrimp, and the method of boiling the shrimp (see pages 3–4) can greatly enhance or detract from the success of Shrimp Remoulade.

Just a word about the "Creole mustard." This is a brown mustard, and in New Orleans recipes it definitely means a specially prepared brown mustard put up by two or three well-known houses. It is highly spiced and contains a much higher percentage of horseradish—and hence has a distinctively spicier taste and sharper bite—than most ordinary brown mustards. Creoles eat this New Orleans mustard full strength, as a sauce in itself, on soup meats and other bland boiled meat dishes, though many visitors find it a bit too strong for their taste. When cut half-and-half with good mayonnaise (not salad dressing), as it is in this recipe, it simply cannot be replaced in making the delicious Remoulade Sauce so popular with all who taste it in the foremost cuisines of New Orleans and the Gulf Coast.

These ingredients make a little over 1 cup sauce. The number it will serve depends on whether it is to be used over cocktail shrimp or whether Shrimp Remoulade will be a full-fledged "fish course." As a cocktail course, it will allow for 6 cocktails, with 2 generous tablespoons of sauce atop each 4-to-6 shrimp portion. If Shrimp Remoulade graces your menu on its own, as it often does in New Orleans, double this recipe for 6 to 8 servings. The shrimp, served 8 to 12 per person, should be well tossed and marinated in the sauce for at least ½ hour before they are piled in a mound on a large salad plate and served literally swimming in the sauce. No lettuce or other salad-like decoration is needed. Only crackers accompany this course, which many New Orleans businessmen order for a flavorful lunch at top-flight restaurants.

Oyster Cocktail

The addition of wine to this oyster cocktail makes it tops, although Jesse says wine is not absolutely essential and insists that the sauce will have "punch" aplenty without it. However, I'm sure you'll like this if you try it, since almost everybody to whom we have served it exclaims on the "different" flavor. For those guests who may not like raw oysters, you can serve this very same sauce over shrimp with equal success. This recipe will serve 8.

6 *tablespoons oyster liquor*
6 *tablespoons tomato catsup*
dash of cayenne pepper
½ *teaspoon cream-style horse-radish*
⅛ *teaspoon garlic salt, or ½ garlic clove put through garlic press*
2 *tablespoons sherry or Burgundy*

¼ *teaspoon Creole mustard*
1 *teaspoon celery pressed through garlic press or chopped extremely fine*
½ *teaspoon grated onion*
¼ *teaspoon sugar*
¼ *teaspoon salt*
⅛ *teaspoon pepper*
1 *teaspoon Worcestershire Sauce*
48 *oysters*

Mix all sauce ingredients together and serve over the oysters. The saltiness of the oysters, oyster liquor, tomato catsup, etc., will have some bearing on how much salt you will need, so add this seasoning last.

Sherried Oysters in Bacon Blankets

Starting off a dinner party with an unusual hors d'oeuvre is excellent strategy on the part of any host or hostess. Once, when I was conducting a column in the *Miami Daily News*, I served these oysters at a newspaper party at which former Governor James M. Cox, publisher and Democratic standard-bearer in 1920, was a guest. The governor, a noted gourmet, was so entranced that he devoured an entire platter of oysters at one sitting.

This recipe will serve 6 ordinary eaters. The oysters must be very hot, so have them ready to bake as the guests gather.

1 qt. oysters	1 tablespoon butter
1 thin slice bacon for each oyster	3 or 4 dashes of Tabasco Sauce
3 oz. (2 jiggers) sherry	3 teaspoons Worcestershire sauce

Select the oysters—the larger, fatter, and fresher the better—either the night before or the morning of your party. Wrap each oyster separately in a thin bacon slice. Secure with a toothpick through bacon and oyster. (Do not use colored toothpicks as the dye will come off.) If the wrapping is done the night before or on the morning of the party, store the oysters in the refrigerator in a glass dish.

Place the oysters in a large pan as close together as possible, even crowding them, because they will shrivel when the heat strikes them. Pour the sherry over the oysters, and dice the butter over them. Shake a little Tabasco sauce over the pan, and sprinkle a few drops of Worcestershire sauce over each oyster.

Place the pan of oysters under a broiler with a moderate flame and cook, turning the oysters occasionally, until the bacon is slightly crisp. If the oysters are not uniform in size, some will brown before others, so watch the broiling process carefully.

The broiling should take no longer than 7 to 10 minutes. Serve immediately with potato chips or other hors d'oeuvres.

Oyster Cutlets

These distinctive and flavorsome appetizers are prime favorites at our home. They literally melt in your mouth. This recipe will produce about 36 cutlets—6 apiece for 6 people. Cooking time is 2 hours, so they should be prepared well in advance of the party.

1 *qt. fresh oysters with their liquor*
½ *cup butter (do not use oleomargarine)*
1 *cup flour*
½ *pt. light cream*
1 *teaspoon prepared mustard*
1 *teaspoon Worcestershire sauce*
2 *teaspoons salt*
pinch of black pepper
dash of cayenne pepper
2 *eggs*
cracker crumbs
fat for frying

Pour the oysters and their liquor into a medium-sized saucepan, place over a low fire, and let them steep until their edges curl. Pour into a colander over another pot to catch the oyster juice. Let the oysters drain well, then transfer them to a wooden chopping bowl and chop them fine.

Prepare a white sauce as follows: Melt ½ cup butter over a low fire. Stir in the flour until smooth; pour in the cream, stirring constantly until the sauce is thick. Add the chopped oysters and stir until well mixed. Add the mustard, Worcestershire sauce, salt, and pepper. Beat 1 egg slightly and add. When the mixture is so thick it can hardly be stirred, smooth it on the bottom of a shallow Pyrex or china platter, about 10 by 14 inches and ½ inch deep (do not use a metal pan). Then place it in the refrigerator for about ½ hour until it hardens. Cut into 1-inch squares and roll them between your hands. Beat the other egg, mix with cracker crumbs, and dip the cutlets in the mixture. Fry them in a basket in deep fat until brown—they will brown almost immediately. Serve hot on individual dishes. The cutlets should be eaten with cocktail forks.

Hog's-Head Cheese Hors d'Oeuvres

Hog's-head cheese, when served cold in 1-inch squares on crisp crackers, is one of the most delicious of all hors d'oeuvres. It may be bought in the markets in the Deep South, but Jesse prefers to make his own, and there is no comparison between the two products.

1 *hog's head (about 8 lbs.)*
4 *pig's feet*
3 *onions*
6 *cloves garlic*
4 *bay leaves*
3 *sprigs fresh thyme*
1 *teaspoon cayenne pepper*

½ *teaspoon black or white pepper*
2 *tablespoons chopped fresh parsley*
2 *tablespoons chopped celery*
1 *tablespoon Worcestershire sauce*

Procure a small fresh hog's head from your butcher. Have him split the head down the middle. Wash it well, cut out the eyes and eardrums, and clean the cavities thoroughly. Put it and the pig's feet in a pot of water to cover. Cut up 1 onion and 3 cloves garlic and add to the water. Bring to a boil, then simmer until the meat begins to fall off the bones—about 3½ to 4 hours. Cooking the meat to this falling-off-the-bone stage is essential for good hog's-head cheese, and old pork may take longer simmering. Take the meat and bones out of the pot and set them aside to cool, saving the water. When cool, take the meat off the bones and cut it up fine. Strain the water the head and feet were boiled in into another pot and add the chopped-up meat. Mince 2 onions and 3 cloves garlic fine and add. Add the rest of the ingredients. Boil until thick. Pour into 12 to 15 soup dishes to thickness of about ¾ inch. When thoroughly cooled, place the cheese in the refrigerator overnight or for at least 2 or 3 hours. Cut into small squares and serve on crisp crackers. If you pour the mixture into deeper (and fewer) bowls, the cheese may be sliced for sandwiches.

Liver Pâté

6 *fairly thick slices liver*
4 *tablespoons butter*
2 *cloves garlic, sliced*
1 *to 2 tablespoons mayonnaise*
dash of cayenne pepper

2 *teaspoons Worcestershire*
  sauce
¼ *teaspoon Creole mustard*
¼ *teaspoon salt (to start)*
⅛ *teaspoon pepper*

Grill the liver in the butter with the garlic for 3 to 5 minutes. Grind the grilled liver in the food chopper, add mayonnaise to make pâté the desired consistency, and add the other ingredients. This should be the consistency of potted ham or other sandwich spread, and is delicious for lunchtime sandwiches or as an appetizer or salad.

❦ 2 ❦

GUMBO AND SOUPS

Creole Gumbo

Like barbecue, Kansas City steaks, Southern fried chicken, and Mexican chili, whose names are often taken in vain in restaurants throughout this land, the culinary miracle of real Creole gumbo gets more than a fair share of abuse even from chefs and cooks who should know better.

Although classified as a soup, genuine Creole gumbo is a meal in itself, and a most delicious and nourishing one. It takes time to prepare and more time to cook, but the results make the operation more than worth the extra effort involved.

Jesse's Creole Gumbo is a triumph of artful blending of a number of what might be termed non-related and even supposedly clashing ingredients. In what other dish, for instance, are ham, veal, chicken, oysters, shrimp, and crabs made to join so harmoniously to produce a flavor almost impossible to describe? If you can procure the components of this magical dish, treat yourself to a feast you will never forget.

This recipe is for 6.

2 *lbs. fresh shrimp (if possible, with the heads still on)*
12 *live bluefin crabs*
3 *slices bacon*
4 *large onions, minced fine*
4 *cloves garlic put through garlic press or minced very fine*
2 *bay leaves*

1 *tablespoon finely chopped green pepper*
pinch of thyme
1½ *teaspoons sugar*
salt and pepper to taste
2 *lbs. fresh or frozen (not canned) okra*
1 *large hambone*

½ lb. chicken wings or same
amount of any leftover chicken

1 lb. boneless stewing veal

1 heaping tablespoon lard

⅓ cup chopped parsley

1 large can tomatoes, or 4 large
fresh tomatoes dipped in hot
water and peeled

3 or 4 liberal dashes Tabasco
Sauce

4 tablespoons Worcestershire
sauce

juice of ½ lemon

1 pt. fresh oysters

Clean the shrimp (see instructions in recipe for Shrimp Creole). Don't cut them up. Put the shells on to boil. Drop the live crabs into boiling water, cook for 5 minutes—no longer—and clean by removing shells, "dead fingers" or lungs, and entrails in center. Break the bodies in half and twist off the fins. Scrape the shells and catch the juices and fat particles from the corners—this is very important for a gumbo. Save the claws.

Fry the bacon in a large pot until crisp, remove, and set aside. Fry the onions until golden brown, add the minced garlic, and fry until it is brown. Add bay leaves, green pepper, thyme, sugar, salt and pepper. Fry slowly until the green pepper is limp. Add the okra and continue cooking until the okra loses its gummy consistency. Put the hambone, chicken, and veal to brown in another pot with the lard. When the meats and the onion mixture have both browned well, pour off about half of the excess grease from each, and then combine the two.

Add the chopped parsley, tomatoes, Tabasco Sauce, Worcestershire sauce, and the lemon juice. Add the crab sections with juice, claws, shrimp, oysters, and bacon, and fill the pot with liquid from the boiled shrimp shells, plus extra water, until the water covers the shrimp, crabs, and meat well. At least 2 quarts of liquid are necessary.

Boil over a slow fire for at least 2 to 2½ hours. Stir occasionally. Overcooking will never hurt Creole gumbo; it blends the flavors that much better. Remove hambone and chicken bones just before serving. Serve over fluffy white rice, in soup plates.

Creole Gumbo Filé

Gumbo filé (pronounced *fee-lay*) is a seasoning and thickening powder made from sassafras and thyme leaves and is used only when fresh crabmeat and okra (two important requirements of a good gumbo) cannot be obtained. Jesse uses gumbo filé only in the winter, when the cold north winds drive the crabs into the mud under Mississippi Sound, and fresh okra disappears from the markets and vegetable stands.

You will need fresh oysters and fresh shrimp for this dish—also, of course, gumbo filé, which is sold in most grocery stores. Here is Jesse's recipe:

1 *lb. fresh or frozen shrimp*
2 *tablespoons lard or fat*
2 *large onions, minced*
3 *cloves garlic, minced*
2 *tablespoons flour*
1 *lb. boneless stewing veal, cut in chunks*
1 *hambone or ½ lb. ham, cut in chunks*
½ *teaspoon pepper*

1 *tablespoon chopped celery*
3 *bay leaves*
½ *teaspoon salt*
1 *tablespoon fresh parsley*
2 *sprigs thyme*
1 *pt. fresh oysters*
2 *tablespoons gumbo filé*
2 *tablespoons Worcestershire sauce*

Shell the shrimp and clean them by removing the black vein at the back with a sharp knife. Put the shells in 2 quarts water and boil for 5 minutes; then strain the water through a colander into another pot. Melt the lard in a Dutch oven or aluminum kettle and brown the minced onions and garlic in it over a slow flame. Stir in the flour and brown it; then add the cut-up veal, ham, pepper, celery, bay leaves, salt, parsley, and thyme. Pour in the water saved from the shrimp shells, add 1 quart water, and boil ½ hour. Add the oysters and shrimp, boil another 15 minutes, then add the filé and Worcestershire sauce. Cook 5 minutes longer. Serve hot over rice. Serves 5 to 7.

Fish Chowder

Fish chowders fall into one of two general categories—those with tomatoes, and those without tomatoes; or Manhattan *vs.* New England. Although chowder is regarded as soup, it really is a full meal in itself and can be served as such, with a simple lettuce-and-tomato salad on the side.

1 *moderately thick fish, or 2 lbs. fish fillets*
¼ *lb. salt pork, diced*
2 *onions, chopped fine*
5 *small raw potatoes, diced*

1 *pt. evaporated milk or fresh milk*
1 *tablespoon butter*
2 *slices toast, diced*
salt and pepper to taste

The first requirement for this flavorsome dish is a moderately thick, comparatively boneless fish, such as sheepshead, red snapper, redfish, or any clear fillet. Pompano is unsurpassed as a chowder fish.

Fillet the fish and cut it into ½-inch cubes. Take out as many bones as you can. Fry the salt pork in an iron or heavy aluminum kettle. When it is crisp, remove the pork and brown the onions in the grease. Add the fish and potatoes and cover with hot water. Simmer until the potatoes are tender. Pour in the milk and 2 cups hot water. Cook for about 5 minutes, then add the butter. Sprinkle the toast on the surface of the chowder. Add salt and pepper to taste, but remember that the salt pork has already added salt to the mixture. Serve in soup plates or bowls. Serves 4.

Bouillabaisse

3 lbs. fish (any good, firm fish for boiling, such as thick slices of good-sized red snapper, sheepshead, redfish, grouper, or green trout) and fish heads

1 teaspoon salt (to start with)

½ teaspoon black pepper

4 whole cloves

6 whole allspice

1 large or 2 small cloves garlic, put through garlic press or chopped very fine

3 medium-to-large onions

1 carrot, sliced fairly thin

2 tablespoons olive oil

2 tablespoons butter

1 sprig or large pinch of thyme

1 large bay leaf, or 2 small ones

1 tablespoon parsley, minced fine

1 stalk celery, minced

1 small can tomatoes or 1 cup chopped fresh tomatoes

pinch of saffron

½ lemon, sliced very thin

12 whole raw oysters

1 cup raw shrimp, peeled and cleaned, or boiled crabmeat, or both

several generous dashes of cayenne pepper or Tabasco Sauce

¼ cup sherry

buttered toast

To begin this complicated dish, which is one of the classic favorites of both Creoles and Louisiana Cajuns, you must make the fish savory. Rub it well with salt and pepper. Crush the cloves and allspice with a potato masher or wooden mallet (this method is much superior to buying spices already ground). Rub the fish thoroughly with this mixture and part of the chopped garlic. Wrap the fish in waxed paper so that it may absorb the fragrance of the spices. Chop 2 onions fairly fine. In a Dutch oven or similar pot, fry the carrot, chopped onions, and the rest of the garlic in olive oil and butter until golden brown. Slice one onion, put it in a pot with about 1 quart water, the thyme, bay leaf, parsley, and celery. Add the fish heads, bring to a boil, and allow to simmer. When the stock has simmered to about 1 pint it is just right. Strain the liquid.

Now you are ready to begin the actual putting together of one of the noblest of the Deep South's Creole fish confections. Lay the seasoned fish slices atop the golden-fried carrot-onion-and-garlic mixture, cover tightly, cook for 10 minutes or so, and then remove the fish. Add the tomatoes and fish stock, and saffron to color the dish the typical Bouillabaisse yellow. Add the lemon slices. Add the oysters, shrimp, and/or crabmeat. Be sure that this brew is now salted and peppered (with both black and cayenne pepper) to taste. Let boil until the liquid is reduced by about one-half, and then lay the fish carefully back in the pot, add the sherry, and let boil for another 5 or 10 minutes. You'll have to watch carefully to see that the fish doesn't overcook to the point where it falls apart; but on the other hand be sure, by testing one fish slice or fillet, that it's cooked all the way through. Half-done fish is never good. To serve, place fish atop well-buttered toast slices and pour sauce over all. This makes 6 to 8 servings.

Shrimp Bisque

Crayfish bisque is traditional in the South, and recipes for it are numerous and varied. But Shrimp Bisque as Jesse does it is, as far as I have observed, entirely original and as unknown to other cookbooks and kitchens as Jesse's Watermelon Sherbet is. Since Jesse usually makes the bisque as a by-product from the liquor in which he cooks shrimp for other purposes, he serves it on a day other than that on which the shrimp themselves are starred on the menu. Besides, he insists that the bisque is always better after having been stored at least 24 hours.

In making it, Jesse takes care not to salt too highly the elaborately seasoned water in which he boils fresh shrimp. (He always uses fresh vegetables, herbs, and condiments rather than the packaged or dried varieties. See the detailed recipe under Showy Shrimp Buffet.) He is also careful not to put too much water in the shrimp-boiling pot, merely covering the shrimp well. When he has cooked the 2 to 3 pounds shrimp and removed them from the seasoned water, Jesse strains the liquor off through a fine sieve, mashing the juice and some of the soft pulp from celery, onions, garlic, and other flavorings through the strainer along with the shrimp water. When he shells the shrimp he removes the heads and puts the heads back into the water and then pounds them with a heavy spoon or masher. After mashing the heads in the liquor, he again presses the liquor through the sieve, forcing as much as possible of the soft pulp through the strainer with the liquid. To make Shrimp Bisque he uses:

1 qt. broth from boiling shrimp
1 can clear consommé or bouillon
juice of ¼ lemon
2 tablespoons Worcestershire sauce
½ cup sherry
boiled shrimp

3 tablespoons butter
1 tablespoon flour
hard-boiled eggs, sliced
fresh lemon
sherry
chopped parsley

To the shrimp broth, Jesse adds the consommé, lemon juice, Worcestershire sauce, and sherry. A few shrimp bodies, peeled and chopped, are added to the bisque, which is then stored in the refrigerator for serving later in the day or within the next few days.

Just before serving, Jesse heats the bisque and slightly (very slightly) thickens it by slowly adding the heated soup to a mixture of butter and flour that has been blended smooth over a low flame. (For 1 quart of soup 1 tablespoon flour blended with 3 tablespoons butter is ample for proper thickening to a thin-broth consistency.) He places in each soup plate a slice of hard-boiled egg, 3 or 4 small or medium-sized whole boiled shrimp (with the heads on), and a ¼-slice wedge cut from a fresh lemon, and ladles the bisque, piping hot, over all. Jesse adds 1 teaspoon sherry to each serving and sprinkles a pinch of chopped parsley over the top immediately before placing the bisque on the table. This recipe serves 4 to 6.

Deep South Corn Soup

2 tablespoons butter
2 tablespoons flour
1 pt. milk
1 pt. bouillon or soup stock

1 can corn, strained through a colander
salt and pepper to taste
popcorn

Melt the butter and stir in the flour; add the milk, bouillon or soup stock, and corn. Season with salt and pepper, boil 5 minutes, and serve in bouillon cups with popcorn floating on top. Serves 4.

❧ 3 ❧

FISH AND SHELLFISH

Baked Redfish or Red Snapper Creole

If you can't find a redfish, buy a red snapper or sheepshead weighing from 5 to 7 pounds. Jesse cleans and scales the fish thoroughly, leaving on the head. Then he prepares a stuffing that is a delicious repast in itself.

STUFFING

1 *lb. fresh or frozen shrimp*
1 *large onion, chopped fine*
2 *cloves garlic, chopped fine*
1 *tablespoon lard*
6 *slices white bread*
1 *small green pepper, chopped fine*
1 *tablespoon fresh parsley*

1 *pt. fresh oysters, chopped*
1 *tablespoon chopped celery*
sprig of thyme
¾ *teaspoon salt (to start)*
¼ *teaspoon black pepper*
1 *bay leaf (whole)*

Shell and clean the shrimp (see page 52) and cut into small pieces. Put the onion and garlic in a frying pan with the lard, and brown for 15 minutes over a low flame. Add the shrimp and sauté for 10 minutes. Dampen the bread and mash it, add to the onions and shrimp, and add the finely chopped green pepper, parsley, oysters, celery, thyme, salt and pepper, and bay leaf. (Do not overdo the green pepper; 1 tablespoonful is ample.) Simmer for 10 minutes, stirring constantly. Place the stuffing inside the fish and sew up the opening with a needle and thread or fasten with skewers.

Preparation of the Creole Sauce in which the fish will bake is next.

CREOLE SAUCE

1 *No. 2 can tomatoes or 4 large fresh tomatoes*	1 *tablespoon lard*
2 *large onions*	1 *sprig thyme*
2 *cloves garlic*	2 *bay leaves*
2 *tablespoons fresh parsley*	1 *tablespoon flour*
1 *green pepper*	4 *slices tomato*
	4 *slices green pepper*

If you use fresh tomatoes place them in hot water for 2 minutes and then remove the skins. Chop the onions, garlic, parsley, and green pepper very fine.

Melt the lard in a skillet over a slow fire, then add the onions, garlic, green pepper, thyme, parsley, and bay leaves. Brown for 15 minutes, then add the flour and let it brown. Now add the tomatoes and let simmer slowly for 10 or 15 minutes.

Place the stuffed fish in a large baking pan and place 4 tomato slices at strategic points on the fish. Put 4 slices of green pepper on the fish also. Pour the sauce into the pan with the fish, cover, and bake in a 350° oven for 30 minutes, basting frequently.

When the fish is cooked, take it out of the baking pan and place it on a large serving platter. Pour sauce over the fish and place the remaining sauce in a gravy bowl. Serve with creamed potatoes, fresh or canned snap beans, and lettuce-and-tomato salad. Serves 6 to 8.

Red Snapper Court Bouillon

Although red snapper is preferable for this famous dish, any fish that will yield thick fillets—such as sheepshead, redfish, green trout, or Florida grouper—can be used. Two things must be kept in mind in preparing court bouillon: the fish must be kept in slices and not allowed to disintegrate; and the gravy or sauce in which it is cooked must be reasonably thick. Large, easily identifiable bones may be left in, but the small bones, if any, should be extracted before the fish is cooked. This recipe will serve 5 to 6.

1 *tablespoon fat or oil*
2 *tablespoons flour, plus flour for dredging*
2 *large onions, minced fine*
3 *cloves garlic, minced*
3 *sprigs parsley*
1 *sprig sweet basil*
generous pinch of thyme

1 *tablespoon Worcestershire sauce*
2 *bay leaves*
1 *No. 2 can tomatoes*
3 *lbs. thick boneless fish fillets*
1 *cup white wine*
salt and pepper to taste

Heat the fat or oil and stir in the 2 tablespoons flour until smooth. Add the very finely minced onions, garlic, parsley, sweet basil, thyme, and Worcestershire sauce. Add the bay leaves whole. When the mixture begins to brown, add the tomatoes and 1 quart water and simmer gently for 15 minutes. Dip the fish in wine, salt and pepper it, dredge each slice with flour, and lay it in the sauce, slice by slice. Cover the pot and simmer the sauce for ½ hour, or until the fish is done. Take out the bay leaves. Serve over a mound of rice with plenty of the thick gravy.

Stingaree Wings Impromptu

There is a common saying that anything that lives in the sea is good to eat. It's pretty hard to believe this holds true with respect to one of the more despised denizens of the Gulf Coast's salty waters, the repulsive and dangerous stingaree, but it does happen to be so.

We've called this recipe "impromptu" because no one would deliberately set out to catch a stingaree for the purpose of cooking it. Stingaree wings will just have to happen to you by accident, as they happened to us, although we had heard for years that the slippery, plate-shaped, spiny-tailed creatures were culinary favorites with the Choctaw Indians, earliest inhabitants of the Coast.

If you manage to snag a good-sized stingaree without getting spined first, kill it with anything handy, then cut off the wings, the outer sections of the body by which the stingaree propels itself. Throw away the center section.

Heat water in a large saucepan and parboil the wings for a few moments, until the skin separates from the flesh. Remove the sections and skin them carefully. Cut them into frying pieces and fry in fat until brown. As the pieces brown, take them from the pan and place on brown paper, salting lightly.

You will find that crisp fried stingaree wings are delicious, with much the same flavor as a New England eel. If your guests don't like the idea of eating stingaree, remind them that it's all the rage now to serve diamond-back rattlesnake on crackers along with the anchovies!

Boiled Sheepshead with Cucumber Sauce

1 4- to 5-lb. sheepshead
3 tablespoons salt
generous sprinkling of black
    pepper
6 whole black peppercorns
20 whole allspice
3 or 4 dashes cayenne pepper or
    Tabasco Sauce

juice and rind of ½ lemon
15 to 20 whole cloves
6 cloves garlic, sliced
2 large onions, sliced
2 large bay leaves
2 large stalks celery, chopped
1 sprig fresh thyme
2 sprigs fresh parsley

BOILING THE FISH

A reasonably large sheepshead—4 to 5 lbs., which will serve four people generously—will require at least 2 to 3 quarts of water, since the fish should be boiled whole with the head on. You need a big enough pan so that you can lift the fish out without breaking the flesh. A large roasting pan will do nicely, although when you learn how delicious boiled fish can be, you will probably want to add to your kitchen a regular fish-boiling pan equipped with a removable section which holds the fish and enables it to be lifted out easily when done.

Prepare the water for boiling the fish by adding 1½ tablespoons salt to each quart. Add the rest of the ingredients, except for the fish. Bring the water to a boil and simmer for 20 minutes.

Place the fish in the water, bring the water back to a boil, then allow to simmer for 15 to 20 minutes. Turn the fish once during simmering—the water should cover it or you will not be able to turn it easily. After 15 minutes, test with a fork to see if the flesh leaves the bones easily. Do not overcook; it will fall apart and become soggy if cooked only a few minutes too long.

Remove the fish carefully to a platter, garnish with lettuce or parsley, and serve with Cucumber Sauce or Shrimp Sauce.

CUCUMBER SAUCE

½ pt. heavy cream

dash of Tabasco Sauce

dash of black pepper

¼ teaspoon sugar

salt to taste

2 tablespoons vinegar

1 cucumber, peeled, minced fine, and well drained

Have the ingredients very cold. Beat the cream until thickened (not too stiff). Add Tabasco Sauce, black pepper, sugar, and salt (a good pinch is sufficient). Continue beating the cream while adding the vinegar gradually. Fold in the minced cucumber.

SHRIMP SAUCE

This delicious sauce is excellent served over boiled fish. It is good with broiled fish too, but not as piquant a taste treat as when the fish is properly boiled. It should never be served with fried fish; the two simply don't go together.

1 cup shelled, cleaned shrimp

1½ to 2 tablespoons flour

2 tablespoons butter

3 oz. sherry

Boil the shelled, cleaned shrimp about 10 minutes in just enough water to cover. Chop the shrimp fine and set aside. Combine the water left from the shrimp with 1 cup liquor from boiling a fish. (This liquor can be removed from the pot during boiling of the fish.) Blend the flour and butter over a low flame until smooth and add slowly the hot shrimp-and-fish liquors. Simmer, stirring constantly until thick, for about 10 minutes. Add the sherry and the minced shrimp and let simmer, stirring occasionally, for another 10 minutes. Serve hot over fish. If desired, you may add a small amount of fresh or evaporated milk to whiten the sauce, at the time you add the wine and shrimps. If the sauce is not to be served immediately, set it over hot water.

Speckled Trout Amandine

This is a favorite old French Creole dish, featured on almost every menu where fried fish—most especially fried speckled trout—is offered. It is a rich and delicious way of quickly converting ordinary fried fish into a company dish worthy of the most discriminating palate at literally only a few extra minutes' notice. Jesse has accomplished it with pan-fried or broiled filleted fish and says that the recipe is as adaptable to almost any fryable fish as to the gourmet's favorite, speckled trout.

6 fillets speckled trout, fried   *2 tablespoons butter*
½ lb. almonds   *juice of ½ lemon*

The trout may be deliciously fried if it is first soaked in a small quantity of milk. Slice 2 cloves garlic and add to the milk about ½ hour before adding the fish. Flavor the milk with salt, pepper, and a small onion, scraped. After soaking, the fish should be rolled in flour and fried in deep fat.

A half-pound of almonds will garnish fish for 5 or 6 persons. Simply chop the almonds to the size used for fudge or other candy, and brown them in a small saucepan in the butter, until the nuts are a rich golden color. Squeeze the juice from ½ lemon into the butter just before serving, and then pile the nuts over individual servings of the fish; or if the fillets are served at the table from the platter, serve from a gravy boat, spooning the sauce over the fish. Serves 4 to 6.

Broiled Green Trout Amandine

The green trout (large-mouthed black bass), the king of Louisiana and Gulf Coast fresh-water fish, is caught in lakes and bayous and ranges in size from ½ pound to 8 pounds. It should be broiled with head and tail left on, but of course thoroughly cleaned and scaled. The sauce is poured over it just before serving.

1 2-*lb. green trout*	¼ *cup finely chopped blanched*
salt and pepper	*almonds*
4 *tablespoons butter or oleomar-*	1 *thick slice lemon*
garine, plus butter for broiling	*parsley for garnishing*

Salt and pepper the fish well, insert a piece of butter or margarine inside it, and be sure the broiler pan is heavily greased under the fish to prevent sticking. Dot the fish with butter or lay a couple of slices of bacon over it. Broil under a low flame so that the fish cooks through by the time its tail begins to curl and brown. A 2-pound fish should take 12 to 15 minutes to broil.

Brown the almonds slowly in 1 tablespoon butter. Meanwhile, brown 3 tablespoons butter, shaking the pan over a low flame until the water is out of the butter and it begins to turn brown and bubble silently. At this point squeeze a section of the slice of lemon into the butter and then drop the lemon slice into the butter. Allow the froth to settle and add the almonds in the butter in which they were browned. Serve immediately over the broiled fish.

Fried Tenderloin of Trout

The word "tenderloin" as used here is a common expression in New Orleans and on the Gulf Coast, and trout fillets are seldom referred to in any other way.

This is an excellent way to prepare speckled sea trout, a perennial favorite on the Gulf Coast. Three large trout, filleted, will serve about 6 people.

3 *large speckled sea trout, filleted*   *cornmeal or fish-fry meal*
salt and pepper   *cooking oil or lard*

Wash the fish, salt and pepper the pieces, and roll them in cornmeal or fish-fry meal. Fill a frying pan half to capacity with cooking oil or lard. Let the oil get hot but not smoking. Fry the fish until brown and serve immediately with Tartar Sauce.

Jesse's Tartar Sauces

There are few fish, no matter how delicious, which a good sauce will not improve. Here's one way Jesse makes Tartar Sauce, which he says is his "everyday" version:

TARTAR SAUCE I

yolks of 2 hard-boiled eggs   1 *tablespoon vinegar*
½ *cup salad oil*   1 *tablespoon mayonnaise*
1 *teaspoon French mustard*   *dash of red pepper*
½ *teaspoon salt*   1 *tablespoon minced onion*
1 *tablespoon minced sweet pickles*

Stir the egg yolks in a bowl until smooth, drop the oil in slowly, and stir in the mustard and salt. Add the pickles and

vinegar. Stir in the mayonnaise and add the red pepper and
minced onion. Stir the mixture well and serve in individual cups
with fish.

TARTAR SAUCE II

This version, using capers, is the one Jesse insists on for party
occasions or formal dinners or luncheons.

½ *small onion*
½ *to ¾ cup mayonnaise*
2 *to 3 teaspoons capers*
2 *or 3 pickles, chopped fine*

green olives, chopped
fresh parsley, chopped
1 *tablespoon red-wine vinegar*

Scrape the onion into the mayonnaise. Add the capers, the
chopped pickles, olives, parsley, and red wine vinegar, and mix
all ingredients well.

Broiled Catfish with Shrimp Sauce

Fried catfish is a traditional Deep South specialty, usually prepared from steaks cut from gigantic "river cats" or "blue cats," the fresh-water variety that inhabits the rivers and bayous of the Southern states from Texas through Florida. But broiled catfish I haven't seen anywhere outside our own home, where my husband and I sincerely believe it is one of Jesse's prize fish dishes. In fact, we are constantly amazed that more persons have never tried to broil catfish, the meat of which, when prepared as directed here, can hardly be distinguished from that of pompano. We prepare ours from the "gaff-top" catfish that inhabit the Gulf Coast's brackish bayous and even stray into the salt-water bays and Mississippi Sound. This fish should not be confused with the "hardhead" or "mudcat" variety, which abounds in this region and is the most renowned and abhorred of all bait-stealers hereabouts. Baby river cats are also delicious when broiled according to Jesse's formula. Here's the method.

4 small "gaff-top" or fresh-water blue catfish, 1½ to 2 lbs. each
salt and pepper
½ cup butter
2½ tablespoons cooking oil
2 or 3 large or medium-sized shrimp, cleaned, cooked, and chopped
½ small onion, scraped
2 tablespoons celery, chopped

dash of Tabasco Sauce
1 medium-sized can sliced mushrooms
1 heaping tablespoon flour
juice from ½ lemon
2 tablespoons Worcestershire sauce
⅓ cup sherry
1 tablespoon parsley, chopped fine

Save the shrimp heads and shells from cleaning the shrimp. Skin the fish and split them and salt and pepper thoroughly. Melt 2 tablespoons butter with 2½ tablespoons cooking oil in a shallow baking pan. Place the fish in the pan. (Be sure the oil has been spread well over the bottom of the pan before placing the fish therein, as this will prevent the fish from sticking to the pan as it cooks.) Dot the top of the fish with softened butter and spread the butter over the fish well with a knife. Place the pan under a very low flame and broil the fish slowly, spooning the butter sauce over it occasionally. When the fish is golden brown all over (without turning), it is well done, if you have not allowed it to brown too quickly under too high a flame.

While the fish is broiling, prepare a sauce by boiling the shrimp heads and shells in about 1 cup water, along with the onion, celery, and Tabasco Sauce. Add the mushrooms and mushroom liquor. Let simmer. Remove the shrimp hulls and heads, being sure to squeeze all juice from them while removing them. Blend the remains of the ½ cup butter with the flour over low heat, and slowly add the shrimp stock, onion and all, to this mixture, stirring to prevent lumping. Add the chopped shrimp, lemon juice, Worcestershire sauce, and sherry. Simmer until slightly thickened (this should not be as thick as the usual heavy cream sauce). Just before serving, mix with the juices left in the broiler pan and stir well. Add chopped parsley. Serve in a gravy boat along with the fish. Serves 3 or 4, depending on the fish-eaters you serve.

Stuffed Gulf Coast Flounder

The Gulf Coast flounder, flat as it is, is an excellent fish for stuffing, and is remarkably delicious when stuffed and broiled, as Jesse does it, with a "mixed-seafood" dressing.

If you can't get the crabmeat and shrimp, however, or if you or your guests happen to be allergic to shellfish, or if the occasion isn't quite gala enough to warrant this special purchase for flounder-stuffing, merely use 2 medium-sized cans of mushrooms instead of the crabmeat and shrimp, and add, if necessary, a few more breadcrumbs to fill.

It is hardly necessary to add that the almonds and wine may also be dispensed with. However, both are quite desirable and lift a stuffed flounder out of the ranks of everyday cookery to the realms of Jesse's raved-about masterpieces.

Jesse insists that you understand one thing about this recipe —do *not* stint on the butter, and he *means* butter. Flounder is essentially a dry fish and needs butter. Skimp on other things in this recipe, but use about ¼ pound of butter. Jesse uses butter substitutes in lots of his cooking, but not in fish sauces.

1 *medium-sized onion, minced fine*
8 *tablespoons butter*
2 *stalks celery, diced fine*
¼ *green pepper, chopped fine*
several fresh shrimp, shelled and cleaned
1 *small can chopped mushrooms*
½ *lb. boiled crabmeat*
scant pinch of thyme leaves
1 *small bay leaf*
1 *tablespoon Worcestershire sauce*

¼ *lb. almonds, browned and chopped fine (optional)*
½ *cup cream or canned milk breadcrumbs*
salt and pepper
3 *oz. sherry or white wine, plus ½ oz. for basting*
2 *fresh flounders, 2 to 2½ lbs. each, or 4 small ones (not frozen)*
2 *tablespoons cooking oil*
juice of ½ lemon

Sauté the finely chopped onion in 4 tablespoons butter until the onion is soft and brown; add celery and pepper and sauté 2 or 3 minutes longer. Add shrimp and mushrooms (with their liquor) and sauté until the shrimp are pink. Then add crab-meat, thyme, bay leaf, Worcestershire sauce, almonds, cream, and enough breadcrumbs to hold the whole thing together or to stretch the dressing to desired proportions (according to variations in fish size). Use as few breadcrumbs as you can, and the stuffing will be the better for it. Salt and pepper to taste. Add the sherry or white wine, and stuff the fish. Close the slits with the aid of small skewers and lace up. Heat 2 generous tablespoons cooking oil along with a large lump (at least 2 tablespoons) butter in a broiler pan, and place the fish in the pan.

Broil the fish *slowly* under a *low* flame, spooning a bit of the butter over them (add a bit more if necessary) from time to time as they cook. As the fish begin to brown, add a jigger of sherry or white wine (whichever you used in your stuffing) to the broiler pan to increase basting liquid and keep the fish moist. This also adds a delightful flavor to the flounder itself. It is not necessary to turn the fish. Just keep the broiler pan as far from the flame as possible and the flame as low as possible, and when the top is golden brown or slightly darker, the fish will be cooked through.

Serve on individual plates or on a serving platter garnished with lemon slices and lettuce leaves or parsley. Spoon the sauce from the pan over the fish, and sprinkle with the juice from ½ lemon. Serves 4.

Pompano en Papillote

Pompano en Papillote has become the byword for New Orleans culinary splendor, famed among natives and visitors and in practically all of the better-known eating houses there. But curiously enough this picturesque and flavorful method for preparing one of the Deep South's most prized of all table fish, the Florida pompano, is not really an old Creole family favorite. Of fairly recent origin, it was introduced around the turn of the century or shortly thereafter, probably by some of the fresh-from-Paris chefs who so jealously guarded their secret that only in recent times was the papillote method for cooking fish used anywhere except in New Orleans' most famous restaurant cuisines. Old Creole family cooks were not familiar with the dish, and old Creole cookbooks make no reference to it, simply but firmly stating that the only way to enjoy pompano is to broil it in butter and season it with a dash of fresh lemon juice and a sprinkling of chopped parsley just before serving.

So Jesse's recipe for this very tempting method for serving pompano-in-the-bag—which is the way to say it in English—is therefore not a generation-to-generation old family formula or an original dish, as most of these recipes are. This particular presentation ought to be especially interesting to readers of this book because it represents concrete proof that this elaborate sort of Deep South cookery can be easily duplicated by non-Creoles—and even by non-Southerners. Jesse's Pompano en Papillote, as you see it described here, is his slightly modified version of a prized formula presented to my husband and me by Lawrence Taylor, a former Yankee, now one of the Gulf Coast's leading restaurateurs, whose Town House in Gulfport, Mississippi, is one of this section's leading restaurants, noted especially for its seafood masterpieces. We have all agreed that Lawrence's presentation of Pompano en Papillote is one of the most delicious and successful of any of the many formulas we have tried for reproducing this popular star of the typical New Orleans French restaurant's menu. Here's how it's done, as slightly modified by Jesse in the light of his varied experience.

3 medium-sized pompano (you can't be choosy as to this fish's size; you take whatever pompano you can get and cut or stretch your stuffing to accommodate them)

3 slices bacon

3 or 4 shallots, chopped, or 1 medium-to-large onion, chopped fine

2 stalks celery, chopped

1 green pepper, chopped

1 medium-sized can sliced mushrooms

1 can truffles (a second can of mushrooms may be substituted, but truffles are traditional)

1 tablespoon flour

3 oz. white wine

salt and pepper

2 cups boiled crabmeat (not frozen)

3 or 4 boiled shrimp, chopped fine

chopped parsley

2 egg yolks, beaten well

1 tablespoon Worcestershire sauce

Fillet the pompano. Save the bones and the cleaned heads. Parboil the fillets 8 to 10 minutes in a small amount of water. Remove the fillets, and simmer the bones and cleaned heads in the same water. Strain and set aside the water for use as stock in the sauce. (You should have about a pint of this stock, so if you use too much water, reduce it by boiling.)

Fry the bacon slices until crisp and set aside. Sauté the onion, celery, and green pepper in the bacon grease until they are tender and light brown (not dark or crisp or too dry). Add the mushrooms and truffles, sauté a minute or two, and then add the flour and stir to blend well. After several minutes, add the warm stock slowly and stir to blend smooth. Stir in the white wine. Salt and pepper to taste. Crumble the bacon. When the sauce is completely smooth and beginning to thicken, add the crabmeat, shrimp, bacon, and parsley. Mix well. Allow to cool slightly and pour slowly into the beaten egg yolks. Add the Worcestershire sauce. Place over a low flame and allow to thicken.

Place the fish fillets on individual squares or lengths of heavy brown paper (cut 12 by 18 inches) which have been generously greased with butter. Use the fish fillets and crab filling as if preparing sandwiches, with the filling spread between fillets. Seal the bags by folding them as if making and closing envelopes; place them in a well-greased pan, flap-side down, to keep juices from escaping while baking. Bake at 375° for 20 to 25 minutes to complete the cooking of the fish. Serve in the closed bags, and break them open at table. This recipe will serve 6.

Oysters Rockefeller

This provides enough for 6 persons to have 6 oysters apiece as an opening fish course at a party dinner. If Oysters Rockefeller are served as a main course, any oyster fan worth his salt will need 10 or 12 as a portion.

36 oysters on the half shell
1¼ cups sour cream
½ teaspoon salt
several dashes of Tabasco Sauce or cayenne pepper
1 teaspoon garlic crushed in garlic press
1½ teaspoons lemon juice
1¼ cups fresh spinach, minced fine
coarse salt (the kind used for freezing ice cream)

6 slices bacon
4 green onion tops, chopped very fine (or 4 tablespoons scraped onion)
2 tablespoons parsley, chopped fine
½ cup grated Parmesan cheese
4 green celery leaves, chopped fine, or 1 teaspoon celery salt
¾ cup butter
¾ cup breadcrumbs
salt and pepper to taste

Be sure to cut the muscles joining the oysters to the shells, and remove the oysters from the shells entirely. Blend well together the sour cream, salt, Tabasco Sauce, crushed garlic, and lemon juice.

Boil about two-thirds of the chopped spinach 6 or 8 minutes in a small amount of liquid, preferably oyster liquor. Set aside.

Next fill the bottoms of shallow baking pans with coarse ice-cream salt and heat in a moderate oven until salt has become very hot. While the salt is heating, brown the bacon in a small pan until it is thoroughly crisp, then chop it or mash it with a fork until it is the consistency of very fine crumbs. Mix in the pre-cooked spinach, chopped onion tops, parsley, cheese, celery leaves, butter, and some of the breadcrumbs, saving part of the crumbs for later use. Heat slightly to melt the butter and bacon fat. Blend well and season with salt and pepper.

Remove the salt pans from the oven. Put a liberal spoonful of the first mixture (sour cream, salt, garlic, lemon juice, and Tabasco) into each oyster shell, and arrange the shells on the hot salt bed. Run the pans back into the oven for 5 minutes, or time enough to get the garlic sauce piping hot. Remove the pans again and place an oyster in each shell. Place a heaping spoonful of the second mixture (bacon, cooked spinach, chopped onion tops, etc.) on top of each oyster. Sprinkle each with a bit of chopped raw spinach. Top off with a light dusting of breadcrumbs mixed with a small pat of butter and a bit of grated cheese, and dot with butter the size of a large pea. Once more put back in the oven and bake for 10 to 12 minutes or until the oysters curl up at the edges. Serve hot on salt beds.

Arnaud's Oysters Bienville

One of the greatest of this country's gastronomical greats was New Orleans' Count Arnaud Cazeneuve. The famed old restaurant which bears his name—Arnaud's on Bienville Street in the Old French Quarter—is still prominent among the city's finest eating establishments.

My father and the count were lifelong friends, so quite naturally our kitchen gained its ample share of the flavor and zest of the count's illustrious cuisine. By all odds the most priceless gem to come our way from Arnaud's is the following formula for Oysters Bienville, an Arnaud original still served as a stellar specialty of that house. My father and most of his gourmet friends vastly preferred Oysters Bienville to the older and better-known Oysters Rockefeller. Our readers are cordially invited to judge the excellence of my father's gastronomical preference.

By special permission of Count Arnaud's daughter, Germaine Cazeneuve Wells, under whose able management Arnaud's continues in her father's tradition, we present this recipe exactly as it is prepared for her patrons. I think discriminating cooks will understand that we give the recipe with tremendous pride and even with a certain degree of culinary reverence.

24 to 36 large, fat oysters in the half shell

1 bunch shallots, or 2 large yellow onions, chopped very fine

¼ lb. butter

2 to 3 tablespoons flour

1 pt. chicken broth or fish broth, scalded

1½ lbs. boiled shrimp, cleaned and chopped very fine

1 can mushrooms, chopped fine

3 egg yolks

3 oz. white wine (Sauterne type)

½ cup light cream or evaporated milk

salt, pepper, and cayenne pepper or Tabasco Sauce

¼ cup breadcrumbs, ¼ cup grated Parmesan cheese, and ⅛ teaspoon paprika, blended together

Place the oysters, in their half shells, in a 375° to 400° oven and bake about 10 minutes or slightly longer—just until they curl around the edges. Take them out of the oven and set aside.

Make a chicken-shrimp-mushroom-wine sauce as follows: Brown the very finely chopped onion or shallots in butter, stirring constantly, until they are golden. Do this gently, so as not to crisp them but keep them juicy and soft. Then add the flour. (Since you will add liquor from partly baked oysters to the sauce, the amount of flour will vary slightly according to the size and number of the oysters. The sauce should be moderately thick, so we advise that you start with 2 heaping tablespoons of flour and add a bit more later if necessary.) Stir over a low flame until the mixture is smooth and brown. Slowly add the broth, which should be heated to the scalding, not boiling, point. (Fish broth is excellent with this.) Add chopped shrimp and mushrooms. Simmer until the sauce is smooth and beginning to thicken. Then set aside the sauce and allow it to cool slightly.

Beat the egg yolks well (but not too much) along with the wine and the cream or evaporated milk. Then *slowly* pour the warm sauce into the egg-wine-cream mixture, stirring and beating constantly to keep the mixture smooth and avoid curdling. At this point add liquor from the pre-baked oyster shells and season to taste with salt, white or black pepper, and a dash of cayenne or Tabasco Sauce. Replace on fire and allow to cook over a low flame for 10 to 15 minutes, or until well thickened, stirring constantly to prevent lumping or scorching. (A tiny bit more flour may be added if the sauce seems too thin.)

When the sauce is thick, pour or spoon it carefully over each oyster and sprinkle well with the cheese-breadcrumb-paprika mixture, to form a fairly thick cover. Place the shells in a 400° oven until the tops begin to turn golden brown. Serve at once.

At Arnaud's these half-shell oysters are always served on a bed of hot rock salt in the style of Oysters Rockefeller.

The usual dinner serving for Oysters Bienville is 6 to a person. This recipe provides enough sauce for 24 to 36 oysters (or more, if necessary); that is, it will serve 4 to 6 persons.

Roasted Oysters in the Half-Shell

This is one of the finest of all ways to prepare fresh oysters. In New Orleans and along the Gulf Coast oysters may be bought very reasonably by the sack—each sack containing 12 dozen or so oysters. Allow 12 to 18 oysters, depending on the size and succulence, to each person, and serve piping hot right out of the oven with cole slaw, hot biscuits, and corn on the cob.

oysters
crisp crackers, broken up fine
salt and pepper

Worcestershire sauce
fresh lemon juice
butter

If you open the oysters yourself, leave each oyster in the deep half of the shell. Place the oysters in large flat pans, packing them as close together as possible. Sprinkle the cracker crumbs generously over each oyster. Salt and pepper each oyster lightly, add a drop of Worcestershire sauce and a dash of fresh lemon juice. Dot the oysters with butter and place them under the broiler flame or in a hot oven. When the edges are curled—in about 10 minutes—they are ready to serve. Serve on plates direct from the oven or, if possible, in individual pans. They must be eaten hot, and the perfect hostess will keep them coming, a few at a time, until all are consumed. Oyster connoisseurs eat the oysters with oyster-cocktail forks, then drink the flavorsome juice from the shells.

Boiled Crabs

Crabs play an important part in the cookery of most New Orleans and Gulf Coast families. They are plentiful in the summer months and are delicious when boiled and picked with the fingers.

Jesse never uses a "crab boil" or packaged mixture of spices manufactured especially for boiling crabs and shrimp. He makes his own mix.

2 tablespoons chopped celery
1 cup salt
1 tablespoon black pepper
1 tablespoon hot red pepper
4 whole cloves
4 bay leaves
3 sprigs thyme
2 tablespoons parsley, minced
6 whole allspice
12 live blue crabs

Put 1 gallon water in a large pot, add the celery and all the seasoning, and let come to a boil. Drop the live crabs in one by one. Boil for 15 minutes, take the pot off the fire, and let stand for 15 minutes. Pour off the water. The crabs will still be quite warm, and must be further cooled before serving. They are best served "fresh boiled," at room temperature, but are delicious, too, served cold from the refrigerator. Serve on platters at table with nutcrackers to crack the claws. Louisianians usually eat the crabmeat plain; others like to dip segments of the meat in French dressing or cocktail sauce.

Fried Soft-Shell Crabs

Soft-shell crabs are best when they have been purchased alive and kicking, dropped into boiling water, cleaned, and prepared immediately. They may, however, be stored overnight in the refrigerator. Do not freeze them.

2 to 4 soft-shell crabs
1 scant cup milk (fresh or evaporated)
salt and pepper
1 level teaspoon sugar
dash of Tabasco Sauce

1 small onion
2 cloves garlic
flour
baking powder
fat for frying

To clean, lift the soft shell on the back and remove the lungs or "dead fingers" and entrails in the center of the crab. Do not remove the shell. To enough milk to cover the crabs, add salt and pepper to taste, the sugar, and Tabasco Sauce. Scrape the onion into the milk (slice the last of it into the mixture), and cube the garlic and add it. (The amount of milk you use depends on the size and number of the crabs.) Soak the crabs in this mixture for 40 minutes to 1 hour—the longer the better. Just before frying, put flour and a few pinches of baking powder into a paper bag and shake the crabs in it gently so as not to dislodge the loosened shells or the claws. Fry the crabs immediately in hot fat, turning them once or twice if necessary. When they are golden brown, take them out of the fat and drain them on paper placed on a hot plate. Tartar sauce is delicious with soft-shell crabs, but some gourmets prefer them plain.

Stuffed Crabs

A good stuffed crab should be spicy and moderately hot, but not too torridly seasoned, as too much pepper will destroy the delicate crab flavor. If you can procure live blue crabs, pick the meat out yourself. If live crabs are not available, use iced but not frozen fresh crabmeat. A dozen medium-sized crabs will yield about 1 pound of meat and stuff 8 crab shells.

If you use live crabs, save the shells for stuffing with crabmeat. If such shells are not available, use Pyrex crab shells.

2 *large onions, minced fine*
3 *cloves garlic, minced fine*
1 *tablespoon lard, melted*
1 *lb. crabmeat*
1 *tablespoon minced parsley*
2 *bay leaves*
1 *tablespoon salt*
½ *teaspoon Worcestershire sauce*
½ *teaspoon cayenne pepper*
sprig of thyme
1 *tablespoon chopped celery*
6 *slices toast*
1 *egg*
¼ *cup evaporated milk*
butter

Fry the onions and garlic in lard until brown, then add the crabmeat, all seasoning, and the celery. Let fry for 10 or 15 minutes. Wet the toast with water, squeeze in the hand to remove excess water, and add; beat the egg and add it, stirring well. Add the milk and stir until the mixture is dry. Place it in shells, dot with butter, and brown in a 350° oven for 10 or 15 minutes.

Crab and Noodles Creole

This is a Florida version of Creole cookery, designed to bring out the delicate flavor and aroma of the bluefin crab. Its success depends on the amount of crabmeat used, and also on the tang lent the dish by frying some of the crab sections in fat. This recipe will serve 5 to 6.

12 *large fat live crabs*	1 *No. 2 can tomatoes*
1 *tablespoon fat or olive oil*	1 *teaspoon salt, or salt to taste*
1 *large onion, minced*	1 *teaspoon sugar*
3 *cloves garlic, minced*	1 *teaspoon Worcestershire sauce*
1 *tablespoon chopped green*	1 *teaspoon vinegar*
pepper	*dash of cayenne pepper*
1 *tablespoon flour*	2 *1-lb. packages egg noodles*

Bring a large pot of water to a boil, drop the live crabs into it, and boil for a few minutes until they turn pink. Drain off the water and let the crabs cool. Clean them by snapping off the claws and legs and removing backs, "dead fingers," and entrails in center. Break the crab bodies into halves, pick the meat from the bodies of six crabs, and set aside in a small pan.

Fry the halved bodies of the remaining six crabs, and all the claws, in fat or oil in a Dutch oven or heavy aluminum kettle. When they are browned, remove from the pot and set aside. Brown the onion and garlic in the same oil, add the green pepper, and cook until the pepper is limp but not black. Stir in the flour until smooth. Add the tomatoes, salt, sugar, Worcestershire sauce, vinegar, and cayenne. Simmer 15 to 20 minutes. Boil the noodles in a separate pot, following directions on the package. When they are done, pour into a colander and drain. Set aside. Add the browned crab sections and claws to the simmering sauce, add the picked crabmeat, carefully removing any pieces of shell. Simmer 30 to 40 minutes over a low flame. Add the noodles just before serving, mixing well through the sauce. Be sure to let the mixture bubble a bit so that it is thoroughly hot. Serve in a large bowl, giving each person a portion of crab sections and claws along with the noodles. Serve with a green or lettuce-and-tomato salad.

Creamed Crabmeat

Creamed crabmeat may be served either from a casserole, on toast, or in individual ramekins. Serves 6.

4 *tablespoons butter*
2 *tablespoons flour*
½ *pt. light cream*
1 *tablespoon minced parsley*
1 *teaspoon salt, or salt to taste*

⅛ *teaspoon black pepper*
dash of cayenne pepper
1 *lb. fresh crabmeat*
½ *teaspoon Worcestershire sauce*

Melt the butter in a pan, stir in the flour, and add the cream, stirring until smooth. Add minced parsley, salt, and cayenne. Add the crabmeat, stirring until thoroughly mixed. Add the Worcestershire sauce. Serve on toast or put in ramekins and heat in a moderate oven for 10 minutes.

Crab Stew Creole

This savory dish may be made with either fresh boiled crabmeat or with meat from live blue crabs, although the flavor will be much better if you use the latter. One pound of crabmeat is usually the yield from 6 to 8 large crabs. This recipe will serve 7 or 8.

6 *large live crabs or 12 small crabs (or 1 lb. fresh crabmeat)*
3 *tablespoons lard*
2 *large onions, chopped fine*
3 *cloves garlic, chopped fine*
3 *tablespoons flour*
1 *sprig thyme*
2 *bay leaves*
1 *tablespoon fresh parsley, chopped fine*
1 *tablespoon celery, chopped fine*
salt and pepper to taste
1 *tablespoon Worcestershire sauce*

Drop the live crabs in a pot of boiling water and parboil them for 2 or 3 minutes, just enough to kill them. Pour off the water, let the crabs cool, snap the claws off, and remove the "apron," "dead fingers," and entrails.

Put the lard to melt in a pot over a low fire, add the onions and garlic, and let fry slowly until brown. Add the flour, stirring until it is brown. Cut the crabs in half, add to the mixture with the rest of the ingredients and 2 cups water. Let cook slowly 30 minutes. Serve with boiled rice. The popular way of consuming crab stew is to pick the meat from the crab sections with the fingers.

Cheesed Crabflakes en Coquilles

My mother used to tell us that this was the favorite recipe of Mrs. Ernest Thompson-Seton, wife of the famous naturalist and author, and a noted lecturer, author, and artist in her own right. It has become one of Jesse's standbys, and Jesse insists that if you boil the crabs for it yourself, seasoning the water according to directions given on page 41, the results will be ten times better than if you use canned boiled crab, although this too is delicious indeed. If you can't get either of these varieties, pass the dish up entirely, for frozen crab, in Jesse's opinion, wouldn't taste so good, and he fears the excess water might interfere with the correct frying of the crab balls. (He feels so strongly on the subject that this opinion is based only on his guess. He simply won't use frozen crabmeat at all.)

2 eggs
meat from 1 dozen large crabs
   (¾ lb.), boiled
salt and pepper to taste

dash of Tabasco Sauce
½ cup grated sharp cheese
breadcrumbs
fat for frying

Beat the 2 eggs separately and mix one with the meat from the boiled crabs. Season with salt, pepper, and Tabasco, and stir the grated cheese in well. Sift into this mixture enough breadcrumbs to make the mixture hold together. Form into balls, dip in beaten egg, then in breadcrumbs, and fry in boiling fat to golden-brown crispness. Serve in crab shells which have been boiled, scrubbed, and then dried, or in the Pyrex shells now available in department stores. A tiny sprig of parsley atop each crabflake ball, and lettuce arranged with lemon slices, can make this a tempting and colorful party luncheon entrée. Serves 6.

Crab Omelet

The secret of making a good omelet is, first, to have an omelet pan to cook it in. The best results cannot be obtained consistently from an ordinary flat frying pan. An omelet pan, procurable at most hardware and department stores, is not just a plain round frying pan, but a double-jointed article, semicircular in shape and so constructed that the omelet can be enclosed in two pans which fold together so that the omelet can be cooked or baked alternately on each side.

Remember that crabmeat is not adaptable to freezing. When it is frozen it crystallizes, and when it thaws the crab juices run out and only the tasteless fiber is left. So either get the iced-down product, or pick your own meat from crabs parboiled in hot water.

Jesse's crab omelet is the most popular of his omelets. It was standard fare for Sunday mornings at our home and always delicious.

3 onions, minced
3 cloves garlic, minced fine
6 tablespoons lard
1 lb. fresh crabmeat, either white or dark
½ teaspoon white or black pepper
2 tablespoons celery, cut up fine
2 tablespoons parsley, cut up fine
8 eggs

Put the onions and garlic in lard in a saucepan and let fry slowly until brown. Put in the crabmeat and cook for 10 minutes. Put in the seasoning, celery, and parsley. Beat eggs well in a large bowl until they are frothy. Let the crabmeat mixture cool, pour it into the bowl with the eggs, stir well. Place the mixture in a greased omelet pan, put on a slow fire and cook, turning the pan over every 5 minutes. Serve with Drawn Butter Sauce. Serves 4.

Lobster Thermidor

This is one of the regal dishes of the South. Either Maine or Florida lobsters may be used.

6 *large live lobsters*
2 *cloves garlic, chopped*
1 *onion, chopped*
½ *cup salt*
2 *teaspoons pepper*
¾ *cup butter, plus 3 level table-spoons butter*
½ *cup flour*

1½ *cups fresh light cream*
9 *canned mushrooms, cut up*
⅜ *teaspoon French mustard*
3 *tablespoons chopped fresh parsley*
1 *cup sherry*
3 *dashes paprika*
Parmesan cheese

Put the lobsters to boil for 30 minutes in a pot of water seasoned with the garlic, onion, salt, and pepper. Let cool, remove from the pot, and cut in half. Remove the meat from tails and claws or "feelers." Dice and set aside. Save the shells.

Melt ¾ cup butter in a pot, add the flour, and stir until smooth. Add the cream and stir until the sauce is thick. Take off the heat and set aside. Sauté the lobster meat and mushrooms in 3 tablespoons butter for 5 minutes. Add the lobster meat and mushrooms, mustard, and parsley to the cream sauce, stir for 5 minutes, then add the sherry and stir in well. Add paprika, then place the mixture in lobster shells, sprinkle with Parmesan cheese, put in a 450° oven, and bake for 15 minutes. Serves 6.

Lobster Newburg

(FOR CHAFING DISH)

Jesse makes no secret of where the recipe for his Lobster Newburg originated. In the margin of a yellowed page of the long-out-of-print *Economy Administration Cookbook,* wherein the leading ladies of Capitol Hill more than twoscore years ago offered their choicest family recipes, appears my mother's penciled comment, "Fine!!" The two exclamation points are hers. She thus applauded the recipe for Lobster Newburg by one Mrs. Duncan U. Fletcher, of Jacksonville, Florida, wife of the then United States Senator from that state. Although throughout the years Jesse, on his own initiative or on directives from Mother, tried other variations on the Newburg theme, he says this one remained their favorite, as simple to make as it sounds, and as delicious as Mother's comment indicates.

meat from 2 lobster tails,
  chopped coarse or cut into
  small pieces (not shredded or
  mashed)
4 tablespoons butter
4 tablespoons sherry

2 tablespoons Worcestershire
  sauce
1 tablespoon flour
1½ cups cream
3 egg yolks, well beaten
salt and pepper to taste

Simmer together the lobster, 2 tablespoons (heaping ones) butter, sherry, and Worcestershire sauce for 15 or 20 minutes. In a separate pan melt 2 tablespoons butter and rub into this 1 heaping tablespoon flour until both are smoothly blended. Warm the cream gently (not until it is scalding or boiling hot), and work it into the butter and flour. Remove from the heat and fold in the beaten egg yolks. Cook over low flame in the top of a double boiler until smooth, and pour over the lobster. Heat thoroughly in a chafing dish and serve immediately. Serves 2.

Jesse has often warned me that cream or milk should be warm

when added to a butter-flour mixture, to prevent "lumping" in any white sauce, and this one, of course, is no exception. Also, though most recipes merely advise adding egg yolks to sauces, without further comment, Jesse insists that if any mixture to which eggs are to be added is allowed to cool slightly before the eggs are stirred in, curdling never results. It's a little more trouble, but if you pour the warm mixture slowly into the egg yolks, stirring continuously, and then put the new pot on the fire to cook the sauce (instead of pouring the eggs into the warm mixture and a hot pan), you'll be surprised at how little curdling you'll ever get in any egg-thickened sauce such as this one. It will be rich, mellow, golden yellow, and smooth as velvet.

Either Maine or Florida lobster is adaptable to this recipe, as are crabs or shrimps.

Shrimp Creole Louisiana

To those who have never been initiated into real native Creole cookery, the idea of Shrimp Creole suggests a few dejected-looking shrimp swimming in a thin red tomato sauce liberally strewn with segments of half-cooked onions and green peppers, with a tablespoon of rice thrown in for good measure. As a matter of fact, genuine Creole sauce is neither thin nor red. It is reddish-brown in color and moderately thick in consistency, and the ingredients are minced so fine, cooked so thoroughly, and blended so well that all combine into one ineffable flavor.

It is just as important that the shrimp themselves be suited to the occasion. Do not use canned shrimp. Jesse would rather cut off the hand that has stirred so many delectable concoctions than use canned shrimp in any dish or than precook the shrimp to give them a "pink color." He makes this delightful dish with raw shrimp only, but he states that the frozen headless variety can be used. Frozen crabmeat, never! But freezing seems to help shrimp.

2½ lbs. whole fresh shrimp, or 2 lbs. headless shrimp, fresh or frozen

3 slices bacon, or 2 tablespoons lard

2 large or 3 small onions, minced fine

3 cloves garlic, minced fine or put through garlic press

½ large sweet pepper, minced very fine

1 sprig fresh thyme, or 1 good pinch dried thyme leaves

1½ tablespoons flour

2 bay leaves

1 teaspoon salt

½ teaspoon black pepper

1 teaspoon sugar

2 dashes Tabasco Sauce

1 tablespoon minced celery

1 large can tomatoes or 4 fresh tomatoes (if fresh tomatoes are used, peel by immersing in hot water for 2 minutes, then removing skin)

1 tablespoon Worcestershire sauce

2 tablespoons minced fresh parsley

3 or 4 whole allspice

Jesse really prefers, if it is at all possible, to get fresh shrimp with the heads on. If you can obtain 2½ pounds of fresh whole shrimp, twist the heads off and remove the shells from the bodies. Cover the heads and shells with water in a small pot, place over a low flame, and allow them to boil while you are preparing the rest of the ingredients. Clean the shrimp by slitting them down the back with a small sharp knife and removing the vein at the back with the fingers; or, easier still, float the vein out by shaking the slit shrimp under running water in the kitchen sink or in a bowl of water which you empty at intervals during the cleaning.

Dice the bacon and fry it until crisp, then remove it from the pan; or melt the lard. Fry the onions slowly in the fat until they are limp and brown. As the onions brown, add the garlic and sweet pepper. Fry the mixture for 5 minutes, add thyme, flour (stirring into mixture), bay leaves, salt, pepper, sugar, and Tabasco Sauce. Then add the celery and allow to simmer only a few minutes before adding the shrimp. Continue simmering until the shrimp turn pink; then add the tomatoes, Worcestershire sauce, parsley, and allspice. With a potato masher or large spoon press in a sieve the shrimp heads, shells, and liquor so that the fleshy parts and juice are mashed through, leaving the shells. Add ½ to 1 cup of this juice to the sauce. Simmer 30 to 40 minutes until the sauce has thickened to gravy consistency. Save the extra shrimp liquor to thin the sauce if necessary.

If shrimps with heads on are not available, boil the shells and use water from them. Serve sauce and shrimps over rice, with lettuce-and-tomato salad. Serves 4 to 6.

Butterfly Shrimp

The haunting, evanescent suspicion of onion and garlic in these unusual fried shrimp keeps everybody coming back and back again for more and more. It is amazing what a tremendous difference this simple variation makes in a dish so popular in its everyday form.

4 *to 5 lbs. shrimp*
1 *large onion or 2 small onions*
1 *to 1½ pts. evaporated milk*
4 *large or 5 small cloves garlic,*
    cubed
dash of Tabasco Sauce

1 *teaspoon sugar*
ground black pepper
1½ *teaspoons salt*
flour
¾ *teaspoon baking powder*
fat for frying

In cleaning the shrimp, follow directions (page 52) for removing shells and vein down the back, *except* that you should not remove the entire shell. Leave the last segment and the tail intact. Then slit each shrimp lengthwise through the body down to the last segment of shell, leaving two long strips of flesh hanging loose. These curl back when the shrimp is placed in the hot deep fat, and the tail fans out, so that the cooked shrimp has the appearance of a large golden butterfly. The slitting also allows the crispy coating to cover more of the shrimp than if the shrimp were fried without slitting.

Jesse fries shrimp, as he does soft-shelled crabs, after he has first marinated them in a liquor made by scraping a large onion into canned or evaporated milk (enough to cover the shrimp in a medium mixing bowl); adding cubed garlic (pieces should be large enough so that the garlic flavors the milk but doesn't cling to the shrimp and get fried with them by mistake), and Tabasco Sauce, sugar, and pepper and salt to give a zesty flavor. The milk should be just a trifle saltier than seems necessary, as this salt has to flavor the flour which coats the shrimp too.

When the shrimp have marinated in this milk mixture for

at least 1 hour—preferably a good deal longer—Jesse drops a few at a time into a paper bag into which he has placed flour with a couple of pinches of baking powder added. He changes the bag every once in a while as the flour becomes damp; otherwise, he says, his "butterflies won't fly." He means that the shrimp coating would be soggy and heavy instead of light and crisp.

He then fries the shrimp in deep hot fat. Butterfly shrimp should be served piping hot, preferably as they are cooked, but for formal occasions they can be fried and placed on a paper-covered platter and kept hot in a low oven. Serve with cole slaw, creamed potatoes, and buttered cauliflower. The shrimp may be dipped in Roquefort Shrimp Sauce (page 5) or Tartar Sauce (see pages 28–29), served in a cup on the plate.

Shrimp Jambalaya

An old standby in Creole cookery. Fresh oysters may be substituted for the shrimp.

3 tablespoons lard
2 onions, chopped fine
2 cloves garlic, chopped fine
1 slice (about ½ lb.) cured ham, diced
1 No. 2 can tomatoes
2½ cups raw rice
1 lb. fresh or frozen cleaned, uncooked shrimp (or 1 pt. oysters)

2 bay leaves
1 sprig thyme
1 tablespoon chopped fresh parsley
½ tablespoon chopped celery
salt and pepper to taste
dash of cayenne pepper
1 teaspoon sugar

Melt the lard in a pot—preferably of heavy iron or aluminum —brown the onions and garlic, then add the ham. Let the ham sauté with the onions and garlic for 5 minutes, then add the tomatoes and let cook for 3 minutes. Wash the rice thoroughly and place in the pot. Add the shrimp or oysters and the bay leaves, thyme, parsley, celery, and seasonings, and let cook slowly about 45 minutes. Salt and pepper to taste. Serves 6 or 7.

Louisiana Crawfish

The Louisiana crawfish (not to be confused with the Florida rock lobster) is a critter found in swamps, sloughs, and roadside ditches—in fact, one may even build a home in your back yard—which seems like a cross between a Maine lobster and a Florida crawfish (lobster), but in miniature. Louisianians capture them in ditches and sloughs by dragging chunks of meat over the bottom and retrieving them periodically, usually with the crustaceans clinging to them. Louisiana crawfish are sold in the summertime along the roadsides near New Orleans by the bucketful, and they are delicious if properly cleaned and cooked and dunked in a cocktail sauce.

Here are the ingredients for a real crawfish "boil." To consume it in the approved manner, everyone should strip to shirtsleeves and eat as many as he or she can hold.

1 *cup salt*	2 *sprigs thyme*
1 *10-qt. bucket live crawfish*	3 *bay leaves*
6 *cloves garlic*	3 *tablespoons minced parsley*
3 *large onions*	2 *tablespoons cayenne pepper*

Fill a washtub with water and pour in 1 cup salt. Mix the salt into the water, then drop in the live crawfish. The crawfish will swim around for a while, and the salt water will cause them to purge themselves of mud and impurities. Meanwhile cut up the garlic and onions, put about 2 gallons of water in a large pot, add the garlic, onions, and all the remaining ingredients. Boil the water for 15 minutes. Drop in the crawfish and boil for 20 minutes. Turn off the heat but let the crawfish remain in the water for 10 minutes. Take the crawfish out and place in a large pan until cooled, then serve with cocktail sauce or Sweet French Dressing. Serves 2 or 3 native Louisiana crawfish eaters, 4 to 6 amateurs.

Enchilado

This recipe is one of my husband's mother's old favorites from Key West. Bijol is imitation saffron, which can be purchased in most Key West stores. It will color the dish a rich yellow and give it a pungent flavor—though not so decided a one as true saffron. Because it is less expensive than true saffron, we use bijol almost invariably.

1 *large onion, or 2 small onions, chopped*
4 *cloves garlic, minced*
1 *sweet green pepper, chopped*
¼ to ½ *cup olive oil*
1 *can tomato sauce*
1 *can tomato paste*
1 *teaspoon orégano*
1 *teaspoon paprika*
1 *small package bijol (optional)*
1 *large bay leaf*
salt, white pepper, and red pepper to taste
stone crabs, blue crabs, crawfish, or shrimp enough to provide helpings for 4

Fry the onion and garlic and green pepper slowly in the olive oil until they are a little past the golden-brown stage. Add the tomato sauce and paste and all the seasonings. Simmer until the sauce is thick and well blended. Add the crawfish, crabs, or shrimp, raw. (Do *not* boil the shellfish before putting them in the sauce. Take them out of the shells raw and cut the meat into small pieces.) Simmer the fish in the sauce for 20 minutes or ½ hour, till they are thoroughly cooked and the water from them has bubbled away, leaving the sauce velvety thick.

Serve over rice or with a vegetable.

❦ 4 ❧

POULTRY

Roast Turkey with Oyster Stuffing

1 10- to 14-lb. turkey
salt and pepper
2 large onions
2 cloves garlic
1 tablespoon fat
1 pt. oysters
turkey giblets, cut up fine
6 slices toasted bread

1 tablespoon chopped celery
1 tablespoon minced scallions
1 sprig thyme
1 tablespoon fresh parsley
2 bay leaves, crushed
1 lb. lard or oleomargarine
flour

Clean and wash the turkey inside and out, rub salt and pepper inside and out. Make a stuffing as follows.

Mince the onions and garlic and brown in the fat. Place the oysters in hot water until the edges curl, then pour off the water but save it. Chop the oysters fine. Put the oysters and giblets in the pot with the onions and garlic and let fry 15 minutes. Soak the toast in the oyster water and mash it. Add to the onions and garlic. Add the celery, scallions, thyme, parsley, bay leaves, and salt and pepper to taste. Stuff the turkey and fasten the opening with thread or skewers. Grease the turkey with lard and sprinkle it with flour. Put 1 pound lard or oleomargarine in the baking pan (no water). Bake 2 hours, starting the bird breast down, and turning when back and wings are brown, in a 350° oven.

Vol-au-Vent of Chicken

Vol-au-vent—fly in the wind! As typically Old French in flavoring and daintiness as the name implies is this old New Orleans favorite. The name really refers to the air-light pastry shell that encases a succulent filling of chicken, oysters, or other such delicacy. Heavy meat fillings should, of course, never be used in the Vol-au-Vent.

The pastry shell and its cover are baked beforehand. The filling is poured into the shell, and the Vol-au-Vent is then placed in the oven for quick warming and immediate serving, before the lighter-than-air crust has had time to absorb too much gravy and become soggy. You will note that the crust for this masterpiece is a slightly modified version of the recipe for Jesse's Old-Fashioned Piecrust, which is used for ordinary meat potpies.

The basic trick of Vol-au-Vent is *not to allow the dough, especially the shortening in it, to get warm.* If the shortening gets warm during the mixing, the grease will melt through the flour instead of staying in lumps or flakes. Cold, hard shortening flakes and lumps are an absolute *must* for successful puff paste. Therefore, Vol-au-Vent is best reserved for cool weather, unless you make it, as so many modern Orleanians do nowadays, in pastry shells prepared by a bakery that specializes in puff paste (or, to use a better-known term, patty shells).

The following delicious Vol-au-Vent filling, which Jesse borrowed from the cuisine of Corinne Dunbar's Tearoom in New Orleans, may be served in individual patty shells. But as Vol-au-Vent, which is the true New Orleans way, it is always served in one oversized shell, which can be made to order by most confectioners who make the smaller shells. So, if you prefer perfect results the first time, rather than hazarding a try at the puff paste yourself, order a Vol-au-Vent shell 12 inches long, 8 inches across,

and 2½ inches deep for the following filling, which is made from
a treasured old recipe.

2 *stalks celery*
2 *large onions*
4 *cloves garlic*
3 *or 4 sprigs thyme (or several
     small pinches dried thyme)*
1 *young hen (3½ to 4 lbs.)*
¼ *lb. butter*
3 *cups warmed chicken stock*
2 *tablespoons flour*

4 *sprigs parsley, chopped fine*
1 *teaspoon Kitchen Bouquet*
½ *cup Sauterne wine*
2 *small cans butt mushrooms*
salt and pepper
patty shell
*lettuce leaves, parsley, lemon
     slices*

Dice the celery, one of the onions, 2 cloves of garlic, and the
thyme. Boil these, with the young hen, in water to cover, until
the hen is tender. *Boil the chicken slowly;* quick boiling will
toughen the meat, but slow boiling tenderizes it. It should take
from 3 to 4 hours to get the chicken properly tender. Let the
chicken stock cool. Remove the chicken from the pot, take the
meat from the bones, and cut it into small pieces as for Chicken
à la King. Set aside.

Chop fine ½ large onion or 1 medium-sized one (the juicy yellow kind is best) and brown it in the butter, ever so slowly, so
that it stays soft when it turns golden brown. Add 1 large garlic
clove (or 2 small ones), also chopped very fine or put through a
garlic press. Brown slightly. Add the flour and brown a bit more.
Then add 3 cups of warmed chicken stock, the chopped parsley,
and Kitchen Bouquet. Add the cut-up chicken and let simmer until the gravy is thickened. Add the wine and mushrooms. Salt and
pepper to taste—about ½ teaspoon salt and ⅛ teaspoon pepper
will be a good starter.

Just before serving, heat the patty shell thoroughly in the oven
and then pour the hot chicken filling into the shell, and cover
with the top crust of the patty. Serve at once, garnished with
lettuce leaves, parsley, lemon slices or other decorations, on a
large platter. The tasty mixture is spooned from the shell, and a

bit of the top crust is included with each serving. With second helpings, which will always be in demand, divide the lower crust, which by this time is well permeated with the chicken gravy but still crispy and flavorful to the last morsel. This should feed 4 to 6 guests, depending upon occasion and appetites.

VOL-AU-VENT PUFF PASTE

If you are a dauntless soul (as I am), a good pastry cook, or a true gourmet, you will not be satisfied until you have conquered the making of your own Vol-au-Vent shell. To make the delicate puff paste, you will need a fairly deep loaf pan (the heavier the metal the better, but *not* a glass baking dish) and a heavy pastry tin (a heavy skillet will do).

½ *cup butter, plus* ⅛ *lb., ice-cold*
¾ *cup lard*
3 *cups flour (measure after sifting*
4 *times)*

18 *tablespoons ice water*
1 *egg*

In a cold mixing bowl cut the ½ cup butter and the lard into the sifted flour until it is the size of small marbles or large peas. (We *do* mean lard, not vegetable shortening. Jesse insists that good old pork lard mixed with butter makes far better puff paste than either pure butter by itself or butter mixed with any other fat.) Although most cookbooks advise using knives to cut the shortening into the flour, Jesse achieves wonderful results with a light aluminum kitchen spoon, with the edge of which he lightly slices the ice-cold lumps into the flour. Jesse taught me how to do this, working always with an inward-and-upward "scooping" stroke of the spoon, with a short outward-and-upward twist of the wrist; the outer edge of the spoon slices into the flour, not only cutting the shortening lumps but also each time lifting a bit of flour and some pastry lumps, thus introducing more and more air into the flour with each cutting stroke. Jesse particularly cautions against using the spoon with a "mashing" motion that would tend to press or squeeze the grease into the flour rather than flaking it in. I am sure this is one of his top secrets for fine pastry-making, and the method has worked wonders for me in biscuits and rolls as well as puff paste. To keep the butter and lard hard while working, have the bowl very cold before beginning, and then stand it in a pan of ice water while cutting the grease into the flour.

When the shortening has been thoroughly flaked into the flour until it is in lumps of the large-pea size, add 18 tablespoons of ice water, three or four spoonfuls at a time, lightly and quickly mixing it into the flour with the same scooping motion; do not knead or mash with the spoon. Adding the water in such small quantities keeps it colder while mixing and prevents the shortening from melting; also, you avoid "flooding" your dough. The dough should be slightly on the damp side when it is lifted from the bowl; if it is too dry it will not roll out thinly without breaking or cracking.

Jesse never touches dough with his hands except when absolutely necessary—this also helps keep the shortening cold. He lifts the dough from the bowl with the spoon, gently drops it on a lightly floured board, and sifts a light coat of flour atop the lump. Then he rolls the dough out immediately, with no kneading and no waiting, to ¼-inch thickness. He then takes the extra ⅛ pound of butter from the freezer compartment of the refrigerator, where he has let it get very cold (not frozen), and chips small lumps from it to scatter all over the rolled dough, using about half the butter. Then, *very lightly*, he taps the flour sifter over the dough to leave an ever-so-thin dusting of flour over the butter-dotted surface. Next he quickly folds the dough in half and rolls this out slightly. He repeats the butter-dotting procedure and again flips the dough in half (thus having four layers of pastry sandwiched together with floured butter-lumps between them).

The dough is then divided by cutting off a piece equal to one-third of its size, with a sharp knife. Set this aside in the refriger-

ator. The larger portion is lightly rolled out to slightly less than
¼ inch thick and lifted gently into the deep loaf pan, where it is
shaped into position quickly. It is then set in the refrigerator for
2 or 3 hours' chilling. (You can cut down this chilling time by
about one-half by placing it in the freezer compartment.)

When thoroughly chilled, the crust is popped directly from
the refrigerator into a very hot oven—another secret for getting
the biggest rise out of your puff paste. The oven should be well
preheated to 500°. Twelve to 15—perhaps 18—minutes should
be sufficient to brown the puff paste lightly; but the time will
vary slightly according to your oven and the degree of chilling of
the pastry. Be sure to watch this operation carefully, as the shell
will scorch easily because of its high butter content. But allow at
least 5 minutes before opening the oven, to give the paste time to
puff up. If you are sure of your stove temperature, it is even better to wait 8 or 10 minutes before letting cool air into the oven;
even then don't open the oven door wide, but merely take a quick
peek, to avoid making the paste fall.

The smaller portion of the Vol-au-Vent dough, which forms
the top of the shell, is taken from the refrigerator, rolled out to
¼-inch thickness, and shaped to fit the top of the shell—round,
square, or oblong, depending upon the size and shape of the
bottom. It is placed on a pie tin or flat griddle pan, and chilled
and baked in exactly the same manner as the bottom crust.

The Vol-au-Vent shell may be removed from the pan and
filled and topped, then served on a platter; or the serving may be
done from the pan the shell was baked in. The heavier your
baking utensil, the higher your crust will rise, and the easier it is
to remove, I have found. (We use a small iron Dutch oven for the
bottom crust and a heavy aluminum skillet-grill pan for the top.)

You will find that if you put a sheet of waxed paper under the
dough before rolling it you will be able to get the dough safely
into its baking pan a lot more easily than if you try to handle the
dough without the paper.

This recipe is lengthy, but making the puff paste is a lot

simpler than the directions may sound. Without including the little tips and tricks of Jesse's trade, however, I do not think I could recommend Vol-au-Vent making to the average cook. If you follow these directions carefully, step by step, exactly as given here, you will be amazed at the delectable French-type pastry you will take from your oven.

Fried Chicken

1 *large frying chicken, 2½ to*   *fresh or evaporated milk*
  3 lbs.   *fat for frying*
salt and pepper   *flour*

Jesse's fried chicken is one of his greatest culinary triumphs. He cuts up a chicken in quarters and washes the sections well in cold water. He then rubs the pieces with salt and pepper, puts them in a bowl, covers them with fresh or evaporated milk, and lets them soak for 15 minutes.

To fry chicken, Jesse fills a large skillet or Dutch oven with sufficient grease or fat to cover the chicken. When the grease gets hot he dips the sections of chicken in flour and fries them until they turn a golden brown. As he takes the pieces out he puts them in a pan and places them in a low oven (200°) to keep hot.

Chicken fried this way will always be deliciously crisp and succulent. The secret of the crispness is the soaking-in-milk process.

Chicken Royal

Jesse's Fried Chicken is delicious when served "as is" with appropriate vegetables. But a sumptuous variation is his Chicken Royal, in which two sauces blend for a truly festive culinary event.

Frying procedure for the chicken is the same as for Fried Chicken (see page 65); but Chicken Royal is served more elaborately and looks every bit as good as it tastes. A white Sauce Supreme is poured into one end of the serving dish, while a red Tomato Purée Sauce is poured into the other end. The chicken, fried golden brown according to Jesse's wonderful recipe, is placed atop the sauce, and slices of bacon fried "just to the point" —not too crisp or too dry—are crisscrossed over the top of each of the chicken pieces. The whole dish is popped into the oven to heat well before serving. Bouquets of parsley or lettuce, or fried eggplant slices or corn fritters, may be placed on the dish before serving.

SAUCE SUPREME

1 tablespoon chicken fat (or bacon fat)
1 tablespoon butter
1 tablespoon flour

1 pt. chicken broth, boiling
salt and pepper
dash of Tabasco Sauce
pinch of nutmeg

Melt the chicken fat and butter (if you haven't the chicken fat, bacon fat will do) and heat with the flour, stirring until the mixture is smooth and turns yellow. Add the boiling chicken broth (canned chicken soup will do nicely, or you may boil necks and backs from chickens to make the broth). Cook 25 minutes on a very low fire, stirring almost constantly. Strain, add salt and pepper, Tabasco Sauce, and nutmeg.

TOMATO PURÉE SAUCE

1 *hambone*
1 *small onion, chopp ery fine*
1 *stalk celery, choppud very fine*
1 *carrot, chopped very fine*
2 *or 3 tablespoons whole parsley
   leaves*
4 *tablespoons butter*
1 *tablespoon flour*

1 *can tomato sauce*
1 *No. 1 can tomatoes*
1 *bay leaf*
pinch of thyme
several whole allspice
several cloves
dash of Tabasco Sauce
1 *heaping teaspoon sugar*

Place a hambone in a small pan with the chopped onion, celery, carrot, and parsley leaves. Sauté with 4 tablespoons butter until the onion is limp and golden, and stir in a bit of flour (about 1 tablespoon); add the tomato sauce and tomatoes. Drop in the bay leaf, thyme, allspice, cloves, a dash of Tabasco Sauce, and sugar. Simmer for 30 to 40 minutes. Strain before serving.

Stuffed Halves of Chicken

My husband's favorite chicken dish for fishing or camping trips —in fact, one of his favorite chicken dishes for any occasion—is prepared according to a recipe given us by the wife of one of his fishing companions, Mrs. Joseph Rousseau, of Lakeshore, Mississippi. Not only because of the delicious results, but also because the stuffed baked halves of chicken can be packed and reheated conveniently, this is a useful formula to keep handy.

Select 2 large spring chickens, about 2½ pounds each. Cut the chickens down the center of the back. Grease a shallow pan with 2 tablespoons olive oil, and place the halves in it skin side up. Sprinkle them well with salt and pepper. Bake in the oven at 325° for 25 minutes. Remove the chickens from the oven, turn them over, and stuff them.

The following stuffing will fill 4 large halves of chicken. However, it can be stretched to fill 6, if necessary, by the addition of a little bit more bread and ½ to 1 pound of ground calf's liver to the rest of the ingredients.

2 *cloves garlic*
2 *medium-sized onions*
1 *tablespoon parsley*
¼ *cup celery tops, chopped fine*
chicken giblets, heart, and liver
2 *tablespoons olive oil or Wesson oil*

6 *slices stale bread, soaked in water until moist*
1 *can ham spread*
1 *teaspoon salt*
¼ *teaspoon pepper*
¼ *teaspoon thyme leaves*

Grind together fine (or chop very fine) the garlic, onions, parsley, celery tops, and giblets, heart, and liver. Simmer these in the olive oil in a skillet over a low flame for about 10 minutes. Add bread, broken into small pieces. Add ham spread, salt, pepper, and thyme leaves, and mix thoroughly.

Stuff the chicken halves and return them to the same pan in

which they were partly baked, and add ⅓ cup of water to the pan to prevent the chicken from sticking to the bottom. Return to the oven and bake for 20 to 25 minutes more, or until the chicken is tender.

Broiled Chicken

broiling chicken   *oil for broiling*

Split the chicken, rub it well with oil, and broil *on the inside only*. Jesse stresses that this inside broiling is a secret cooks can use to great advantage. In his broiling, the flame never comes in contact with the outside of the chicken at all. He broils the inside under a direct flame until golden brown—about 20 minutes—and then removes the chicken, pan and all, from the broiler and finishes it in the oven. This procedure, he guarantees, provides maximum flavor and juice inside the chicken and insures against the bloody joints and half-done flesh to which poultry eaters object so strenuously when they are served broiled chicken. For the finishing process, the chicken is turned right side up, and the oven set at 250°. When the chicken is golden brown in this slow oven heat—about 2 hours—you can be sure it is ready to serve, tender, juicy, and well done, with a crisp, succulent outside. The cooking time can be cut to about 1¼ hours in a 375° oven, but the very slow method is the best.

Jesse usually serves this with green asparagus bunched about the border of a large platter, adding a touch of color with a strip of pimento over each asparagus bunch. Small bunches of parsley are tucked here and there for garnish, and frequently, for extra color, Jesse places whole broiled tomatoes at each end of the platter.

Buttered Broiled Chicken with Sherry

As piquant and saucy as the winsome Creole belle who bestowed its formula on our family kitchen's repertoire is Jesse's Buttered Broiled Chicken with Sherry. Lelande de Gravelle Lacoste, one of New Orleans' noted music teachers (now of Gulfport, Mississippi), claims that she "couldn't boil water" when she married, but adds that this favorite of her family was the one dish she could prepare, because of its extreme simplicity—a simplicity no one could ever guess from the superb flavor and elaborate appearance of the finished product. The ingredients may be shrunk or stretched according to the number of guests. To make this party chicken dish for 4 you will need:

2 *large, plump, young fryers (2¾ to 3 lbs. each) cut in half for broiling*
salt and pepper
2 *small onions, sliced thin as paper*

¼ *lb. butter, warmed to room temperature*
1 *medium-sized can sliced mushrooms*
about 1 pt. sherry
1 *heaping teaspoonful flour*

Wash the chickens and clean off all the pinfeathers. Salt and pepper liberally inside and out, seasoning well under the wings, and rubbing the salt into the meat thoroughly. Pile the chicken halves on top of one another with onion slices liberally sprinkled sandwich-style between the pieces, so that all sides come in contact with the onion, and wrap in waxed paper. Let stand for 20 minutes to ½ hour. Then rub the chicken halves with soft butter, covering thoroughly, wing-tips and legs especially.

Next place the buttered chicken, skin side up, in a deep broiling or baking pan, tucking all the onion slices underneath the chicken, along with the gizzards and livers. (Be sure to put the necks in too; they help to flavor the sauce.) Broil the chicken halves under a rather slow flame until golden brown. Then remove the pan from the broiler, turn the halves over, and place them so that the cavities are as level as possible to hold the filling and sauce. Fill the cavities with mushrooms (save the mushroom water in a jar for later use), a large piece of butter, and sherry. Put a few small pieces of the onion into each cavity too, but allow most of the onion, along with the giblets, to stay in the sauce below. Then put the pan into a slow oven—about 300° is best, or even as slow as 250°, if you have plenty of time. The more slowly the chicken bakes, the better it will be. However, if you are late and must rush the cooking, 375° won't ruin the dish at all, if you baste it often. At 250° to 300° you don't have to watch the chicken, except for giving it a slight basting every ½ hour or so. As a matter of fact, Lelande Lacoste explained: "I just put it in a very slow oven and go to church, and when I come home from Mass it's ready—just like that!"

Jesse always likes to baste the broilers a bit, especially if the chickens are on the small side, and he also adds a bit more sherry by degrees as the sauce cooks down, splashing the wine into the cavities, over the mushrooms. Just before he removes the chicken from the oven he puts a heaping teaspoonful of flour into a mayonnaise jar, in which he has kept his mushroom liquor, and shakes the jar vigorously until liquor and flour are blended well —a good trick for gravy-thickening, in case you don't already know it! He then pours the mixture into the broiling pan to thicken slightly the piquant sauce that goes beautifully over fluffy rice. If you've had the oven at 300°, the chicken will have turned a shade darker than golden brown in about 1½ hours or 2 hours, and you will know that it is tender, well cooked completely through, with absolutely no bloody joints, and juicier than any other broiled fowl you'll ever put in your own or your family's mouths. It should be served on a platter or on individual plates, mushroom side up, with generous spoonings of the butter-sherry sauce over all and a bit of lettuce, lemon slice, tomato ring, or the like for color. The gravy from such cooking is copious and should accompany the chicken and rice in a bowl or gravy boat.

Chicken Sauté

1 *small spring chicken*
salt and pepper
flour

butter
1 *slice lemon*

Cut the chicken into quarters, salt and pepper it, dip it in flour, and sauté it in butter on a slow fire for 8 to 10 minutes. Heat 4 tablespoons butter in a pan until it foams and begins to turn brown; then squeeze the lemon slice into the butter. Serve this drawn butter sauce over the chicken, with a bit of chopped parsley, or serve it on the side in a sauceboat.

Chicken Sauté, Hungarian Style

1 *small spring chicken*
salt and pepper
paprika
flour
butter

1 *small onion, chopped*
1 *oz. salt pork, diced fine*
1 *cup chicken broth or soup*
2 *tablespoons sour cream—*
  slightly more, if necessary

Cut the chicken into quarters, salt and pepper it, dust with paprika and flour, and fry in butter on both sides until brown —5 to 6 minutes. Brown the onion and pork in a bit of fat. Heat 1 tablespoon butter with 1 teaspoon flour and add to the pork and onion. Add the chicken broth, add the chicken, and let it simmer until tender—30 to 40 minutes. Then add the sour cream and stir well. Let the mixture come to a boil, remove the chicken, and strain the sauce over it.

Chicken Fricassee, Brown Sauce

1 6- or 7-lb. stewing hen, cut up
2 tablespoons lard or bacon fat
3 medium-sized onions, minced
3 cloves garlic, minced
2 tablespoons flour
2 bay leaves, crushed
2 sprigs thyme
2 tablespoons minced parsley

2 teaspoons salt
1 tablespoon minced celery
1 tablespoon Worcestershire sauce
½ teaspoon pepper
dash of cayenne pepper or Tabasco Sauce

The successful chicken fricassee must have plenty of chicken, so get a large stewing hen. Have it cut up at the joints. Save the liver and gizzard. A 6- or 7-pound fowl will serve 6 to 8 dinner guests.

Wash the chicken pieces thoroughly and put in a Dutch oven with the lard or bacon fat. Let simmer until brown, then take the chicken out and set it aside. Brown the minced onion and garlic in grease; stir in and brown the flour. Put the chicken back in the pot with 2 cups water, the bay leaves, thyme, parsley, salt, celery, Worcestershire sauce, and pepper. Chop up the chicken gizzard and liver and add. Cook for 1 hour, or until chicken is tender. Serve in a bowl or tureen, along with the rich gravy, and serve boiled rice as an accompaniment.

Curried Rice and Chicken

1½ cups raw rice
1 large or 2 small fryers, cut as
    for frying
salt and pepper
1 medium-to-large onion, sliced
2 small, tender stalks of celery,
    chopped fine
4 large or 6 small slices of bacon,
    cut into 1-inch squares
1 medium-to-large onion,
    chopped fairly fine

1 large green pepper, diced
2 pimentos, diced
1 medium-sized can sliced mush-
    rooms (optional)
1 heaping tablespoon curry
    powder
5 tablespoons butter (more if
    needed)
2 tablespoons flour
milk

You will find it most convenient to boil the rice (see Jesse's recipe for Fluffy Rice, page 138) the day before if you're cooking this for a Sunday or party dinner. If the rice is already cooked, you can get it ready for the oven while the chicken is boiling.

Wash the chicken and remove the pinfeathers. Place in well salted-and-peppered water—enough to cover the chicken thoroughly—along with the sliced onion and the chopped celery. (I like to use the heart of the celery for this, as the celery should be cooked very tender and remain in the sauce.) Let come to a boil and then simmer until the chicken is well cooked but still firm. (Watch this carefully, as young frying chickens can by no means take the boiling stewing hens do, especially if they are very young or very small or both. They get done in no time at all—20 minutes ought to be ample from the time your pot starts boiling. Very large and heavy fryers might take ½ hour.)

Fry the bacon squares until they are about three-quarters done —not too crisp. Remove from the pan and save. Brown the chopped onion slowly and, as it begins to turn golden, add the diced green pepper and fry till the pepper is limp and tender. Add to the rice. Add the diced pimentos and the mushrooms (save the liquor from these) to the rice and sprinkle the curry powder over all. With a fork, gently lift the rice over and over, mixing all ingredients thoroughly through it. Put the rice into a ring mold and dot generously with butter or margarine (it takes a good 4 tablespoons to do this right), and then bake in a 350° to 375° oven for 20 to 30 minutes.

While the rice ring is in the oven—and it doesn't matter if the rice sits around a bit after baking and has to be heated again—prepare a cream sauce for the chicken. Boil the liquor in which the chicken was cooked down to approximately 1½ or 2 cups of liquid. (This can be done in a hurry by turning up the flame and boiling the stock vigorously for only a few minutes.) Melt 1 tablespoon butter and blend in 2 scant tablespoons flour. Add the hot liquid slowly, stirring till smooth. Add also the liquor from the mushrooms, and a bit of fresh or canned milk to whiten. Simmer, stirring constantly until thickened. Put the chicken in the sauce and allow it to simmer about 10 minutes. If the sauce gets too thick, add a bit more milk, according to your own taste. Remember that you salted and peppered the water well to begin with, and although the chicken has absorbed some of the flavorings, the boiling-down process has probably left plenty of salt and pepper for the sauce. So taste first before adding any more, which may or may not be needed, depending on how much milk you have added.

Turn the rice ring out on a platter and heap the creamed chicken in the center, and at each end if the center won't hold it all. The chicken sauce, when blended with this version of yellow rice, is a taste sensation you will want to repeat often after your first encounter with it. Serves 4.

Baked Spring Chicken with Crab Apples

This wonderful way to bake a young frying-sized chicken may have been discovered by others, but so far I've never seen it come out of any but Jesse's oven, where he says it originated. It is extremely simple and quick to prepare, but has the million-dollar flavor usually obtained only after hours of painstaking labor. Serves 4 to 6.

2 *plump young fryers (2½ to 3 lbs.), whole*
salt and pepper
⅓ *stick (about 2½ tablespoons) butter, plus butter for greasing the chicken*

1 *can spiced crab apples*
⅔ *large onion*
½ *cup white corn sirup*
4 *slices bacon*
¼ *cup sherry*

Clean the chickens of all pinfeathers, wash, and dry. Salt and pepper them thoroughly inside and out. Chicken takes a lot of these seasonings, so do the job well, rubbing the salt and pepper into the skin instead of merely dusting it over the bird. Then grease the chickens inside and out, preferably with butter. Salt and pepper the giblets and drop them inside, along with a generous lump (⅓ stick) of butter. Fill the rest of the cavity with whole spiced crab apples, which come packed in heavy ruby-red sirup. Use ½ can of apples to each chicken. Complete the stuffing by adding ⅓ large onion—not chopped—to each cavity, and then pouring into each opening half of the corn sirup. Hold the chickens by the legs for a few minutes to allow the sirup to permeate the stuffings. Close with skewers and tie shut. Crisscross across the top of each chicken breast 2 slices of bacon, to cover the breast and most of the uppermost sides of the legs. This will keep the young chickens from drying and browning too fast, and also will add extra flavor.

Place the chickens in a baking pan, along with the sirup from the apple can, spices and all. Add the sherry and bake in a slow

(300° to 325°) oven until the chicken is tender and golden brown —about 2 hours—basting occasionally with the spicy sirup. This is wonderful as a party dish, and extra color may be added by serving additional apples arranged on the dish with the chicken. Chicken baked in this manner is also ideal for picnics.

The main reason for adding the corn sirup is that the apples, when baked in the chicken, lose some of their sweetness and are much more delicious when extra sirup is added. The sirup in which they are packed is tart and just sweet enough to provide an ideal sauce for baked chicken.

Chicken in Burgundy

For your Sunday-night one-dish meal—or a main dish to star on any party menu, for that matter—is Jesse's version of a chicken casserole which he says is originally from Texas.

6 *slices bacon*
2 *fryers (2½ to 3 lbs., but tender and plump and young) cut in pieces for frying*
flour to dredge chicken
1 *large onion, chopped fine*
2 *large or 3 small cloves garlic, chopped fine*
1 *can tomato sauce*
1 *teaspoon chili powder (fresh and high-grade; stale or inferior chili can ruin your dish)*

2 *stalks celery, chopped fine, or ½ teaspoon celery flakes, or 1 teaspoon celery seed*
2 *teaspoons paprika*
dash of cayenne pepper or Tabasco Sauce
¼ *teaspoon black pepper*
salt to taste (use ¾ teaspoon at first and add more later, after you've added the wine)
¾ *to 1 cup Burgundy*

Fry the bacon until crisp and remove it from the skillet. Dredge the chicken thoroughly in flour and brown it quickly in the hot bacon fat. Remove the chicken and brown the onion slowly in the remaining grease. Add the garlic as the onion begins to brown, and then put in the tomato sauce and all the other ingredients except the wine. Cook, stirring well, for several minutes on low heat and then add ¾ cup wine and place the bacon and chicken back in the sauce. Let simmer until the chicken is tender and cooked well through—possibly as long as 30 to 40 minutes, depending on the size of the pieces and the age of the chicken—and until the sauce is thickened and smooth. Add a bit more wine from time to time as the sauce cooks, if it is needed to keep the gravy from getting thick or "gooey" before the chicken is done.

Serve with noodles or hominy or rice, as preferred. Green salad is all you'll need for an ample dinner for 6 hungry persons. If it's a "company" dinner and you're serving vegetables, rolls, and dessert, this is ample for 8 servings.

❧ 5 ❧

MEAT AND GAME

Broiled Beef Steak or Veal Steak with Wine-Merchant Sauce

Sauce for the steak should be prepared in advance and kept ready on the stove. This famous sauce will transform a mediocre steak or indifferent chops into a heavenly treat. The recipe will provide a meat sauce for 4 to 5. Cooking time is 1 to 1½ hours.

4 slices bacon
4 tablespoons butter or oleomargarine
2 tablespoons finely chopped onion
½ clove garlic, minced very fine
½ bay leaf
pinch of thyme
1 tablespoon flour
1 can clear consommé
¾ cup Burgundy
salt and pepper to taste
¼ cup finely chopped parsley
3 tablespoons Worcestershire sauce
1 small can mushrooms
1 very thin slice lemon
beef or veal steak

Cook the bacon in a small saucepan until it is deep golden in color. Remove it from the pan and set aside. Add butter or margarine to the bacon grease, then add the onion. Brown the onion over a slow fire until it is golden. Add the garlic, bay leaf, and thyme. When the garlic is slightly browned, add the flour and brown it. Then add the consommé, wine, salt and pepper, bacon, parsley, Worcestershire sauce, and mushrooms. Squeeze the lemon slice into the sauce and add it. Allow to simmer over a low fire until the sauce has thickened and the seasonings have blended—about 1 hour.

Slash the edges of fat on the steak to keep the meat from lumping or curling while being cooked. Dot the meat with butter but do not salt and pepper it until ready to serve, as salting tends to drain the natural juices and make the meat tough. Place the steak in the broiler pan and place under a hot flame in a preheated broiler. Broil from 3 to 5 minutes on each side, depending on the thickness of the steak and on individual taste. If the steak is very fat, drain off the excess fat. Add the steak gravy in the broiler pan to the sauce. Place the steak on a hot platter, pour the sauce over it, and serve at once. Extra sauce may be served in a gravy bowl to pour over mashed or baked potatoes. The sauce will make the steak go much further, as well as adding a distinctive flavor.

Roast Beef

Choice ribs of beef should be roasted 15 minutes per pound for the outer portion to be well done and the center rare. Jesse stresses the importance of cooking the roast in a hot oven "to brown the meat quickly and seal in all the juice and flavor." He feels that a slow oven would tend to "draw out" the juices and blanch the meat, making it tougher and not as flavorful.

5-lb. rib roast of beef
3 cloves garlic, minced, plus
  sliced garlic for stuffing beef
salt and pepper

1 tablespoon lard or fat
2 tablespoons flour
2 onions, minced

Wipe the beef and stuff small slices of garlic into it. Rub salt and pepper into the meat. Grease it with fat and sprinkle with flour. Put the roast in a baking pan, uncovered, with 3 cups water, the onions, garlic, and the rest of the flour. Roast in a hot oven (450°) until the meat is well browned. Baste every 10 minutes. Serves 6.

Jesse's Hamburgers

1 *small onion, cut in half*
1½ *lbs. clear, juicy ground beef*
3 *large cloves garlic, or 4 small ones*

2 *tablespoons mayonnaise*
1 *teaspoon mustard (brown or yellow)*
salt and pepper to taste

Scrape each onion half into the meat until you can't hold the onion any more. (Do *not* put chopped onions into the meat— merely the juice and scraped pulp.) Cut the garlic cloves into large pieces and *count the pieces* before you add them to the meat, as they must come out later. Add mayonnaise, mustard, and salt and pepper. Knead all together well and wrap in oiled paper. Set aside for ½ hour to allow the flavorings, especially the garlic, to penetrate the meat. Just before molding the meat into hamburgers, be sure to squeeze out the garlic chunks, counting them as you remove them, to be sure they're all present and accounted for. Fry in a little fat until the meat is done according to taste. The mayonnaise prevents the hamburgers from getting dry and hard, and the other ingredients add evanescent flavor your family and friends will find hard to identify—and harder still to resist. Serves 4 to 6.

Creole Meat Loaf

You may use good chuck beef, or veal.

6 *tablespoons lard*
3 *onions, minced*
3 *cloves garlic, minced*
2 *bay leaves*
2 *tablespoons parsley, minced*
3 *tablespoons minced sweet pepper*

2 *sprigs thyme, shredded*
2 *tablespoons chopped celery*
½ *teaspoon black pepper*
2½ *lbs. ground beef*
2 *tablespoons flour*
1 *large can tomatoes*
1 *teaspoon sugar*

Melt the lard in a frying pan, brown the onions and garlic. Add the bay leaves, parsley, sweet pepper, thyme, celery, and pepper. Cook slowly for 5 minutes. Take half the mixture out and mix well with the meat. Put the meat in a baking pan, shaping it to the form of the pan. Brown the flour in the frying pan with the rest of the onion mixture, add the tomatoes, and stir over heat for 5 minutes. Add the sugar and pour the mixture over the meat. Bake in 350° oven for 30 minutes. Serves 7 to 8.

Picadillo

This recipe from Key West is an excellent one-dish meal, ample for 3 to 4 persons when served with small portions of rice and a green salad.

2 *fairly good-sized onions, chopped*	1 *lb. ground beef*
1 *very large or 2 small cloves garlic, minced*	⅓ *cup stuffed olives*
	½ *cup raisins*
1 *large green pepper, chopped*	2 *tablespoons capers*
¼ *cup sweet oil*	1 *tablespoon vinegar (preferably red-wine vinegar)*
1 *can tomatoes*	*salt and pepper to taste*

Fry the onions, garlic, and pepper in the oil over a low flame until they are tender and golden. Add the tomatoes and meat and stir briskly with a fork to break up the meat into tiny pieces so that it doesn't cook in lumps. Add the olives, raisins, capers, and vinegar, and then salt and pepper to taste. (If you haven't any wine vinegar, add the regular variety, but if you want an extra-special flavor, use 1½ ounces good Burgundy too.) Continue cooking until the meat is tender and the sauce has boiled down and thickened somewhat.

The Key Westers never serve Picadillo without rice, but it may be served alone or on crisp, buttered toast, with green peas and fried plantains, for a distinctive buffet, dinner, or luncheon dish.

Spaghetti and Beef

Spaghetti is one of our favorite cold-weather dishes. Jesse's Spaghetti and Beef is not only succulent and delicious, but also the only spaghetti dish we have ever encountered where the sauce sticks to the spaghetti. If you read this recipe carefully you will see how Jesse accomplishes this feat of culinary legerdemain. Note that the recipe calls for beef instead of the customary meat balls. It will serve 6 people.

3 lbs. chuck beef	2 teaspoons sugar
6 tablespoons lard or olive oil	1 sprig thyme
2 large onions, chopped fine	2 bay leaves
4 cloves garlic, chopped fine	salt and pepper to taste
3 tablespoons flour	2 12-oz. packages thin spaghetti
2 6-oz. cans tomato paste	1 cup Parmesan cheese (not the
2 tablespoons chopped celery	kind that comes already grated)
2 tablespoons fresh parsley	

Wipe the meat with a damp cloth (this will keep it from popping and sputtering while it browns). Put the lard or olive oil in a Dutch oven or aluminum pot. When the lard melts put in the meat and let it cook until brown. Take the meat out and put in the onions and garlic. Let them cook on a slow fire until brown, or about 15 minutes; then add the flour, stir until it is brown, add the tomato paste, and stir for 5 minutes to eliminate acid. Put the meat back in the pot, add the celery, parsley, sugar, thyme, bay leaves. Cover with water, let the water come to a boil, and simmer for 1½ hours.

Now prepare the spaghetti. Put 4 quarts water to boil with 1 tablespoon salt. When the water is boiling briskly, drop the spaghetti into it. Stir frequently to keep the spaghetti from sticking to the bottom of the pot. The spaghetti should be tender in about 10 minutes.

When the spaghetti is tender put it in a colander and run cold water over it until all the starch is removed. This will take about 5 minutes. When the meat is done, remove it from the pot to a serving platter. Put the spaghetti in the sauce and stir over a low flame for a few minutes until it is thoroughly hot. Grate 1 cup Parmesan cheese and spread it on the spaghetti. The flour will cause the sauce to stick to the spaghetti. Serve the spaghetti in a covered bowl, and serve more cheese in a separate dish, to be sprinkled over individual portions of spaghetti. Hot rolls or garlic French bread, and a lettuce-and-tomato salad go well with this dish.

Unusual Italian Macaroni

This is a spicy dish, easy to prepare, although its actual cooking may take a long time. When done in the pressure cooker, it can be prepared in an hour or so. It is wholesome as well as delicious and can, with a green salad, make a whole meal. Jesse also serves garlic bread with it, since he doesn't use garlic in the gravy.

4 *lbs. shoulder beef*	1 *heaping tablespoon lard*
small piece of salt pork	2 *very large or 4 small onions,*
½ *lb. Holland cheese*	*chopped fairly fine*
salt and pepper	1 *cup tomato catsup*
flour	2 *1-lb. packages macaroni*

Make gashes in the beef roast and stuff in bits of salt pork and some small wedges of cheese. Then salt and pepper the meat thoroughly, rubbing the seasonings in well. Lightly flour the meat and brown it in the lard, then remove it from the pot and brown the onions. Replace the meat and pour the tomato catsup and 2 cups water over the meat. Cover and let cook slowly for 4 or 5 hours or until the meat is tender. (If you cook this in a pressure cooker, you'll need only a scant ¼ cup water, and 35 to 40 minutes at 15 pounds' pressure ought to be ample—depending, of course, on the age and tenderness of your beef.) Meanwhile grate the remaining cheese.

The macaroni takes about 20 minutes to boil and should not be cooked until immediately before you are ready to serve it. When it is tender, place it in a ring around the meat on a platter. Mix 1 heaping teaspoon flour with a tiny bit of water and add to the meat gravy to thicken it. Then ladle the gravy copiously over the meat and macaroni and sprinkle all liberally with grated Holland cheese. Serve extra sauce in a gravy boat, along with a bit of extra cheese, for those who may desire it. Or you may prefer to mix the whole business up in the pot before bringing it to the table. We have always preferred the former method.

Jesse's macaroni, like his spaghetti, is something to write home about, although it's hard to believe that there's such a wide difference in the preparation of the two. This recipe serves 6.

Short Ribs of Beef

The gravy's the thing with well-cooked and well-seasoned short ribs of beef. Here's how Jesse prepares them.

4 to 5 lbs. short ribs of beef
flour
2 tablespoons lard or bacon drip-
     pings
2 large onions, minced
3 cloves garlic, minced
3 bay leaves
2 sprigs thyme

2 tablespoons chopped celery
2 tablespoons fresh parsley,
     chopped fine
1 teaspoon salt, or salt to taste
½ teaspoon black pepper
dash of cayenne pepper
½ teaspoon Worcestershire
     sauce

Wipe the meat with a cloth and roll it in flour. Melt the fat in a Dutch oven or heavy aluminum pot, put in the meat, and roll it over and over while it is cooking, to brown it thoroughly. When the meat is well browned, take it out and set it aside. Brown the onions and garlic slowly over a low flame until soft and golden. Add 2 tablespoons flour and stir constantly until the whole mixture is well browned. Now add 2 cups water and stir until simmering starts. Add the bay leaves, thyme, celery, parsley, salt, pepper, and Worcestershire sauce. Simmer 5 to 10 minutes. Put the meat in a baking pan (a Pyrex dish will do, but Jesse prefers a metal baking pan) and add the sauce, which should almost cover the meat. Bake, uncovered, in a 350° oven for 50 minutes to 1 hour, or until the meat is very tender and the sauce is rich and brown. Variations in oven temperature or in the age or quality of the meat may make a difference in the cooking time, but the cheapest, toughest type of meat, if cooked long enough in this way, will yield a delicious repast for 8 to 10 persons.

Corned Beef with Cottage Cheese Sauce

1 *piece corned beef (6 to 8 lbs.)*
1 *head cabbage, quartered*
½ *lb. cottage cheese*

sour cream
1 *tablespoon chopped chives*
salt and pepper to taste

Put the beef in cold water and cook it slowly for 3½ hours. Drain, place the meat in fresh warm water, and cook until it is done—about 1½ to 2½ hours longer. Boil the cabbage separately during the last ½ hour before the beef is done, so that it is ready to serve when the meat has reached the tender stage.

Add to the cottage cheese enough sour cream to thin it to a light, creamy mixture. Add the chives (they give a zesty tang) and salt and pepper to taste. Serve the sauce separately in a gravy boat. This recipe will serve 6.

Tasty Frankfurter Lunch

frankfurters
American cheese, cut in strips
2 *heaping tablespoons mayonnaise*
1 *tablespoon sweet oil or olive oil*

1 *generous tablespoon Worcestershire sauce*
1 *teaspoon mustard*
dash of cayenne pepper
salt and pepper to taste

Slit the inside curve of each frankfurter almost from end to end, but not quite, and almost all the way through, but not quite. Into the slit insert a stick of American cheese, and press it in firmly. Mix the other ingredients together and, with the tip of a teaspoon, dredge each slit to overflowing with this sauce. Place the frankfurters in a broiler pan and brown them in a moderate oven. Leave them in the oven at least until they are heated thoroughly and the cheese is well melted; then hasten the cooking, if you must, by browning them under the broiler. They will brown nicely, but more slowly, in the oven.

Ragout of Oxtail Supreme

The chief ingredient of this unusual dish may be obtained in most Southern markets. It is cooked all too seldom. This recipe will serve 6.

3 *lbs. oxtail, cut in 2-inch pieces*
flour
2 *tablespoons lard or bacon drippings*
⅓ *cup chopped onions*
3 *cloves garlic, chopped fine*
1 *bunch carrots, diced*
½ *teaspoon salt*
⅛ *teaspoon black pepper*

2 *dashes cayenne pepper*
3 *whole allspice*
⅓ *cup diced celery*
2 *sprigs thyme*
2 *bay leaves*
2 *tablespoons fresh parsley, chopped fine*
1 *tablespoon Worcestershire sauce*

Wash the oxtail, dry it, and dust it with flour. Melt the fat, add the oxtail, brown it, and remove it from the pan. Put the onions and garlic and 1 tablespoon flour in the pan, and fry until these are brown. Add the oxtail, 2 cups water, and all other ingredients, and simmer until the meat is tender—2½ to 3 hours.

Our family has always liked this cooked with the ingredients listed, which produce a fine brown gravy, but, for those who prefer a tomato flavor, one whole fresh tomato may be added with the water. Serve with rice.

Stuffed Veal Pocket

An excellent Sunday dinner. A 6- or 8-pound veal shoulder will serve 7 or 8 guests.

STUFFING

1½ tablespoons lard or fat
2 onions, minced
3 cloves garlic, minced
½ pt. oysters and their liquor, or
   1 cup ground meat
8 slices white bread, toasted
1 teaspoon salt
¼ teaspoon black pepper

6- to 8-*lb.* veal shoulder, boned
2 large onions
3 cloves garlic
1 tablespoon parsley
2 bay leaves
2 sprigs thyme
½ teaspoon salt
dash of black pepper

For the stuffing, melt the lard in a frying pan and brown the onions and garlic in it slowly. Heat the oysters in their liquor until the edges curl. Take the oysters out; save the liquor. Cut up the oysters and add to the onions and garlic. Cook for 5 minutes. Dampen the toast, mash, and add to the onion mixture, stirring well. Add the oyster liquor. Cook the mixture until it is dry, add salt and pepper, and stuff it into the veal pocket. If you use ground meat, add the meat and toast after the onions have browned, and stuff the veal immediately.

Sew up the veal and place it in a baking pan. Cut up 2 large onions, 3 cloves garlic, parsley, bay leaves, and thyme, and add to the pan along with ½ teaspoon salt, pepper, and 3 cups water. Bake in a 350° oven for 2 hours, basting every 10 minutes.

Veal and Pork Chops Creole

Veal and pork, when combined with a perfect sauce, go very well together. This recipe provides a meal that will be long remembered.

6 veal chops	½ teaspoon sugar
6 pork chops	1 teaspoon Worcestershire sauce
4½ tablespoons lard or fat	2 bay leaves
2 onions, minced	1 tablespoon minced parsley
3 cloves garlic, minced	1 tablespoon minced celery
3 tablespoons flour	2 tablespoons minced green
1 large can tomatoes	pepper
2 sprigs thyme	salt and pepper to taste

Wipe the chops with a cloth, melt the fat in a Dutch oven, and let the chops steam until brown. Take them out and set them aside. Put the onions and garlic in the pot, let them brown, and stir in the flour until it is brown. Add the tomatoes and cook 5 minutes. Add the chops and all other ingredients. Simmer for 1 hour. Serve over boiled rice, with fresh green peas or candied yams. Serves 6.

Roast Shoulder of Lamb

A popular, inexpensive main meat course may be achieved with a lamb shoulder.

4- or 5-lb. lamb shoulder	2 tablespoons flour
3 cloves garlic, minced, plus sliced garlic for stuffing lamb	1½ cups milk
1 teaspoon salt	2 large onions, chopped fine
dash of pepper	1 tablespoon chopped parsley
2 onions, sliced	1 tablespoon chopped celery
½ cup vinegar	1 sprig thyme or several generous pinches of thyme leaves
3 tablespoons lard, melted	2 bay leaves

Wipe the lamb with a cloth, pierce it in about eight places with a knife, and stuff the openings with small slices of garlic. Rub with salt and pepper, and pin slices of onion all over it with toothpicks. Pour the vinegar over the lamb and let it soak for 15 minutes.

Take the lamb out of the vinegar, grease it with the lard, sprinkle it with flour, and place in a baking pan with the milk and all other ingredients. Bake in a 450° oven for 1 hour. Serves 4 to 5.

Broiled Lamb Chops

Very little can be done to improve on the succulent flavor of a tender, juicy lamb chop properly browned under a not-too-hot flame in the broiler. However, although it's heresy to say so, I must add that if the lamb chops are small and cut thinner than in the old days (and whose lamb chops aren't, these days?) top-of-the-stove cooking in a moderately thick aluminum grill pan does not only a satisfactory job, but indeed sometimes even a superior one. If you put a liberal amount of butter in a very hot grill pan, add the chops, and then turn down the burner slightly, you will end up with the juiciest, tastiest lamb chops you ever ate. They can be cooked slightly rare, if you like them so, which is a result you can't possibly attain in modern broilers unless the meat is at least ¾ inch to 1 inch thick. If you're a lover of garlic, as most gourmets are, you will enjoy the flavor produced by laying a thin slice of garlic over each chop as it is broiling, letting the garlic brown in the butter when the chops are turned, and removing it before serving.

Savory Lamb Stew

This stew is simple to make and delicious to eat. It is economical, and filling as well. In fact, lamb stew can hardly be beat as a complete meal in itself.

1 *tablespoon fat*	1 *large can tomatoes*
2 *lbs. stewing lamb, cut in pieces*	1 *cup fresh or canned peas*
3 *onions, minced*	*salt and pepper to taste*
3 *cloves garlic, minced*	6 *potatoes, diced*
2 *tablespoons flour*	6 *carrots, diced*

Melt the fat in a large pot and brown the lamb in it for about 20 minutes. Take the lamb out and set aside. Brown the onions and garlic in the fat. Add and brown the flour, add the tomatoes and cook for 5 minutes, then add the lamb and other ingredients. Cook for 1½ hours. Serves 6 to 8.

Lamb and Sausage, Holiday Style

The price of lamb being what it is these days, any recipe to make it go further should be welcomed. The following recipe will serve 4 persons amply.

¼ lb. mushrooms
French dressing
4 shoulder lamb chops
2 tablespoons fat
4 slices canned pineapple
4 medium-sized potatoes, cut in
    ½-inch slices

2 tablespoons butter
½ lb. pork sausage meat (see
    page 95), diced
2 tomatoes, cut in half
1½ teaspoons salt
¼ teaspoon pepper
½ cup pineapple juice

Marinate the mushrooms in French dressing for 1 hour; the marinating helps to preserve the color and adds to the flavor. Brown the lamb chops slightly in hot fat. Place the chops in a 2-quart heat-resistant glass utility dish, and over each chop lay 1 slice pineapple. Arrange the potato slices around the chops; dot with bits of butter. Over the potatoes place the pork sausage. Arrange the tomatoes and mushrooms on top, and put a bit of butter in each mushroom cap. Season the chops, potatoes, and tomatoes with salt and pepper. Pour the pineapple juice over all and bake in a moderate oven, 350°, about 45 minutes.

After removing the dish from the oven, garnish with parsley or watercress, and paprika. Take the glass dish directly to the dining table and serve from the dish onto hot plates, giving each person 1 chop, 1 slice pineapple, and ½ tomato.

Fresh Country Sausage

A favorite breakfast dish. Jesse makes his own pork sausage this way. The recipe makes 18 to 20 sausage cakes.

2 *teaspoons salt*	½ *teaspoon powdered thyme*
½ *teaspoon cayenne pepper*	2 *dashes celery salt*
dash of Tabasco Sauce	2½ *lbs. pork, ground*
3 *teaspoons sage*	½ *lb. veal, ground*
½ *teaspoon black pepper*	1 *scant tablespoon fat or oil*

Put all the seasonings in a bowl and mix and mash well until fine. Put in the meat and mix well. Store in the refrigerator. Shape into balls or patties and fry in the fat. Serve when brown and crisp.

Roast Pork Loin

Have your butcher nick the bone through, so chops can be served. Cooking time for the pork varies according to its size and age. Jesse insists that testing for tenderness with a fork is the best way to be sure the roast is done, and he emphasizes that a heavy loin cut from a young pig will cook to the tender stage faster than a smaller, tougher loin from an older animal.

6 *lbs. pork loin*	2 *large onions, minced*
3 *cloves garlic, plus cut-up garlic*	1 *tablespoon minced celery*
for stuffing pork	1 *tablespoon minced parsley*
salt and pepper to taste	1 *bay leaf*
2 *tablespoons flour*	1 *sprig thyme*

Wipe the pork loin with a cloth and stuff it with small pieces of garlic between the joints. Salt and pepper it and sprinkle it with flour. Put in a baking pan with onions, garlic, celery, parsley, and all seasonings. Add 3 cups water and bake in a 350° oven 2½ to 3½ hours, basting every 10 minutes. Serves 6.

Pork Chops Mexican

This flavorsome and unusual dish is really of Mexican origin, although you would probably never suspect it. It is not highly flavored or peppery, and although it is made with fresh cream and Roquefort cheese, you will not be able to detect the cheese. In spite of the richness of the ingredients—pork, cream, and cheese—the result is easily digested and makes an ideal one-dish meal when served with a fresh green salad for everyday dinners or a party buffet supper. This recipe serves 4.

2 5-oz. packages egg noodles
salt
7 or 8 tender pork chops
½ pt. heavy cream

piece of Roquefort cheese about the size of an egg
⅓ cup evaporated milk (optional)

Boil the noodles in salted water according to directions on the package, and drain in a colander. Fry the pork chops until they are about two-thirds done—just before they brown—over a low flame. The juice from the chops will help flavor the sauce. Pour off excess fat, leaving a little, with the drippings, in the pot. Heat —do not boil—the cream and cheese over a slow fire until the cheese melts. (For an extra touch, you may rinse out the cream container with about ⅓ cup evaporated milk and add it to the cream with a small extra piece of cheese.) Add the cream and cheese mixture to the pork, and simmer for 40 minutes; then add the noodles.

Some cooks prefer to bone a loin of pork and slice the meat so it can be mixed through the noodles. At home we prefer to serve chops, as we think the bones add flavor to the sauce. For buffet suppers, we cut the meat from the bones before adding the noodles, and cut each chop in halves or thirds for easy serving and easy eating. This delectable dish is very practical, since it can be stretched simply by adding a bit more cream and cheese as you add pork chops, keeping in mind the basic proportions.

Smothered Pork Chops

A rich brown gravy, excellent with fried grits or rice, comes with Jesse's smothered pork chops, which he usually serves as a good old family standby.

6 *or 8 pork chops, not too thin*
salt and pepper to taste
flour
2 *tablespoons lard*
3 *large onions, chopped*
1 *clove garlic, minced or put*
   through garlic press

1 *tablespoon minced celery*
1 *tablespoon minced parsley*
1 *sprig fresh thyme (or pinch of*
   canned thyme leaves)
1 *large bay leaf, or 2 small bay*
   leaves

Salt and pepper the chops and dredge them in flour. Fry them slowly in the lard until they are lightly browned. Remove the from the pan. Put the onions in the pan and brown them slov Add the garlic and brown it. Add the celery and cook 5 minu. Add 1 heaping teaspoon flour and stir over heat for several minutes. Replace the chops in the skillet and just cover them with water. Add the parsley, thyme, and bay leaf last. Simmer slowly until the sauce thickens—about 1¼ hours. If the chops seem done before the gravy has thickened to suit you, stir a spoonful of flour into a small bit of water in the bottom of a cup and add to the sauce, which really should not be gooey or gluey, but deep brown and of medium thickness. Serves 4 to 5.

Spareribs and Cabbage

A perennial favorite of many lands, this hearty dish is especially adapted to Creole cookery. This recipe will serve 6 to 7.

3 lbs. spareribs
2 onions, chopped
3 cloves garlic, minced
3 bay leaves
1 teaspoon black or white pepper

1 sprig thyme or generous pinch of thyme leaves
1 tablespoon salt, or salt to taste
1 3-lb. cabbage
3 large potatoes, peeled

Cover the ribs with water, add the onions, garlic, and all seasonings, and boil until tender. Take the ribs from the water (save the water), place them in a baking pan, and brown them in a 450° oven for 15 to 20 minutes. Remove the core from the cabbage and cut it in quarters. Cut the potatoes in quarters. Place the potatoes and cabbage in the water used to cook the spareribs and boil until the potatoes are cooked. Place the ribs on a large platter and arrange the cabbage and potatoes around them.

Pigs' Tails and Turnips

1 tablespoon lard
2 lbs. pigs' tails
2 onions, minced
2 cloves garlic, minced
1 tablespoon flour
1 teaspoon celery, minced

1 teaspoon parsley, minced
1 sprig thyme
¾ teaspoon salt
⅛ teaspoon pepper
1 bay leaf
8 turnips

Melt the lard in a pot. Wash and cut up the pigs' tails and drop them in the hot fat. Let them brown, then take them out and set aside. Brown the onions and garlic in the fat, stir in the flour until it is brown, put the pigs' tails back in the pot with 2 cups water, celery, parsley, and all seasonings. Peel and quarter the turnips, add, and cook until tender. This recipe will serve 4.

Pigs' Knuckles and Sauerkraut

Fresh pigs' knuckles are more flavorsome than the cured kind.

6 *pigs' knuckles*
2 *large onions, minced*
3 *cloves garlic*
2 *tablespoons minced celery*
2 *tablespoons minced parsley*
3 *teaspoons salt*

2 *sprigs thyme or generous pinch of thyme leaves*
¼ *teaspoon black pepper*
2 *bay leaves*
4 *large potatoes, peeled*
1 *large can sauerkraut*

Wash the pigs' knuckles and place them in a pot with 2 quarts water, onions, garlic, celery, parsley, and all seasonings. Boil 3 to 3½ hours, or until the pigs' knuckles are tender and almost fall apart. When the knuckles are done, take them out and set aside. Place the potatoes and sauerkraut in the water and boil until the potatoes are tender. Put the knuckles back in the pot, warm, and serve. Serves 6.

Chitterlings ("Chitlins")

This is a real Deep South dish—you will probably be unable to obtain the "chitlins" unless you live in the Deep South or some other area where pork is raised. This recipe is for boiled chitterlings, but after they are boiled you can serve them in Creole style by following the recipe for Tripe à la Creole. They are also delicious fried in deep fat.

2 *lbs. cut-up chitterlings*
2 *onions, minced*
2 *bay leaves*
2 *sprigs thyme*

½ *teaspoon red pepper*
3 *cloves garlic, minced*
2 *teaspoons salt*
½ *teaspoon black pepper*

Wash the chitterlings and put them to boil in a pot with all the ingredients and 1 quart water. Cook until tender—about 2 hours. Serves 6 to 7.

Stuffed Ham

From the time of my father's childhood comes Jesse's delightful recipe for stuffed ham, a dish that is claimed with equal pride by both Virginia and Maryland as a typical Easter masterpiece. Recipes for it are "handed-down heirlooms" in old families of both these states, where an Easter celebration is never quite complete without this colorful delicacy served cold to crown the Easter night's buffet.

My father would never admit that any ham does quite as well as a Maryland or Virginia ham, though I have been more than satisfied with Jesse's results with almost any of the standard high-grade hams from the nationally advertised packing houses.

To prepare a stuffed ham, which is as wholesome as it is decorative and delicious, you will need:

about 1 peck young cabbage sprouts
2 bunches shallots
2 bunches chives
2 bunches celery (or pretty nearly a boxful of celery seed)
½ teaspoon salt
½ teaspoon black pepper
dash of red pepper
½ teaspoon mustard seed
1 large (9- to 12-lb.) sugar-cured or corned Maryland or Virginia ham or any high-grade sweet ham

Scald the cabbage sprouts to make them tender and then put all the vegetables through the food chopper, using the finest blade. Mix well with salt and pepper and other seasonings.

Remove the skin from the ham and cut deep gashes lengthwise along the whole length of the ham from the shank to the end of the bone. Then slash gashes across the ham about 2 inches apart. Into these gashes stuff firmly as much of the vegetable mixture as the slits will hold, and use the remainder of the dressing (if there is any—and this will depend on the size of the ham) as a covering for the ham. Wrap the dressed ham in cheese-cloth or other thin fabric, and sew it up to prevent the dressing from boiling out. Then put in cold water, enough to cover the ham, and boil until done—usually from 4 to 5 hours, or about 30 minutes to the pound. Remove from the water and let cool before unwrapping.

This should be served cold. When the ham is sliced, colorful patches of the stuffing garnish each slice.

Baked Ham with Wine Sauce

When Jesse makes this dish he always uses a precooked ham because he finds that it is less salty than raw ham. Even though the ham is precooked, he brings it to a boil in three different waters and then cooks it as described—that is, he covers the ham with cold water, brings the water slowly to a boil, and boils it for 10 minutes. He then pours off the water, covers the ham again with cold water, and repeats the process. The third time, he covers the ham with water and allows it to go on cooking.

Jesse never bakes a ham without boiling it first. He insists that this method keeps it from drying out and from being too salty.

1 *precooked ham (family size)*	½ *lb. raisins*
cloves	1 *can clear consommé*
1 *lb. apple butter (not apple-* *sauce)*	1½ *cups sherry*

Boil the ham until it is three-quarters done—about 20 minutes to the pound. Save 1 quart of the water in which it was boiled. Remove the skin and score the fat. Decorate the fat with cloves. Mix the other ingredients together with the 1 quart water and place in a roaster with the ham.

Bake the ham in a 350° oven until it is done and nicely browned—about 1½ hours—basting with the sauce while cooking. This sauce is not only delicious for serving with the hot ham, but thickens on cooling and can be stored indefinitely in the refrigerator and served cold as a relish with fowl or almost any kind of roast meat.

Higado (Key West Liver)

Besides being a delicious and economical way to add liver to the family menu, since it stretches the now-expensive commodity to unusual lengths, Higado was a welcome suggestion made by my husband some months ago when I was advised by my physician (as are so many these days) to eat liver at least three times a week.

Jesse has his own superb method for grilled liver, and also for making a liver pâté for luncheon sandwiches (see page 16); but this recipe, which he calls his "adopted liver dish," was a wonderful addition to my liver-high diet. It is one of the few we have ever seen for cooking raw chopped liver. Even if you don't like liver, try this. Jesse wagers you'll try it again, and soon.

1 *lb. liver*	⅛ *teaspoon pepper*
2 *cloves garlic*	1 *medium-sized bay leaf*
3 *tablespoons wine vinegar (or*	3 *fairly large onions*
1 *tablespoon vinegar and 2*	3 *good-sized green peppers*
tablespoons Burgundy)	½ *cup oil*
¾ *teaspoon salt*	1 *tablespoon flour*

Cut the liver into 1-inch cubes. Mash the garlic and chop it very fine (I like it put through the garlic press). Add vinegar, salt, pepper, and bay leaf. (If you have red-wine vinegar, so much the better.) Pour over the liver and, with a fork, turn the mixture over lightly to mix well. Set aside for 15 or 20 minutes—a bit longer is even better—in a tightly covered dish so that the raw cut liver may absorb the essences and aromas of the flavorings.

Chop the onions and green peppers and cook the onions in the oil until tender. As they are beginning to turn brown, add the peppers and simmer till the peppers are soft. Sprinkle the flour into the hot oil and stir with a spoon until smooth. At this point add the liver mixture and cook for about 2 or 3 minutes over a low flame, stirring to mix thoroughly the liver, flavorings, and vegetables. Cover tightly and allow to steam for 2 minutes, and serve at once. We like ours on toast. This serves 4.

Jesse's variation on this theme substitutes for 2 tablespoons vinegar the same amount of Burgundy wine. But I assure you that the dish is most delectable even if you don't happen to have the wine on the pantry shelf.

Grilled Liver

4 *thick slices calf's liver (at least*   ⅓ *stick butter*
    ½ *inch thick)*   *onion (optional)*
salt and pepper   *olive oil or sweet oil (optional)*

Trim the gristle from the liver, and slit the meat along the edges to prevent curling. Salt and pepper it. Melt the butter on a small griddle or in an iron skillet. The pan should not be too hot and the butter not anywhere near browned. Place the liver slices in the pan and fry for 3 to 5 minutes over low heat, turning so that each side is golden brown. Water which "fries out" as the butter heats and a bit of the juice from the slowly cooking liver will be just enough to keep the liver from getting too brown too quickly, and this method of cooking will result in tender, juicy liver even if it is cooked very well done, which liver should never be, from either a gourmet or a health standpoint.

If Jesse serves onions with liver he simmers them in olive oil or sweet oil and in a separate pan. Butter browns too quickly for correctly slow-frying onions to the tender, golden, juicy stage Jesse's onions always achieve. He also points out that the liver cooks in so much shorter time than the onions that the onions must be started much sooner anyway, and they can go on simmering while the liver is grilling in the butter. (It takes scarcely 7 to 8 minutes to cook even very thick slices of liver if you're going to serve them slightly rare.) Serves 2.

Baked Tongue with Olives

A baked tongue makes a superlative meat course when larded with Parmesan cheese and olives and cooked in a Creole sauce. Here is how Jesse concocts this dish.

1 *large beef tongue, 3 to 4 lbs., or*	3 *cloves garlic*
3 *small tongues*	2 *bay leaves*
1 *small bottle green olives*	1 *sprig thyme*
¼ *lb. Parmesan cheese*	1 *tablespoon fresh parsley*
1 *tablespoon lard*	1 *dash cayenne pepper*
2 *tablespoons flour*	1 *tablespoon salt*
2 *large onions*	½ *teaspoon black pepper*

Parboil the tongue in water to cover for about 30 minutes. Take it out of the water, let it cool, then skin it with a sharp knife.

Remove the olive pits and cut the olives into quarters. Make holes in the tongue and stuff the olives into them. Cut the cheese into strips about the size of cigarettes and stuff these also into the holes. Place the lard in a pot and melt it over a slow fire. Roll the tongue in 1 tablespoon flour and sauté it in the lard for 10 minutes, turning it frequently. Chop the onions and garlic fine, take the tongue out of the pan, and add the onions and garlic to the lard along with 1 tablespoon flour. Let brown slowly. After the mixture has browned, place the tongue in the pot, pour 4 cups cold water over it, add the bay leaves, thyme, parsley, pepper, and salt, and cook over a slow fire for 1 hour or until tender. Take the tongue out of the pot, place it on a platter, and put the gravy in a gravy bowl. Slice the tongue into individual servings, pour the gravy over it, and serve with steamed rice, creamed cauliflower, and Waldorf salad. This recipe will serve 6.

Tripe à la Creole

Tripe is often neglected because of ignorance of a tasty way to prepare it. Jesse's Tripe à la Creole is a very flavorsome concoction if you use fresh tripe. Don't attempt this recipe with the canned product.

6 *tablespoons lard*
2 *lbs. honeycomb tripe*
2 *whole cloves*
2 *large onions, minced*
3 *cloves garlic, minced*
2 *tablespoons flour*
1 *large can tomatoes*
1 *tablespoon sugar*

2 *bay leaves*
1 *tablespoon fresh parsley*
1 *sweet pepper, minced*
2 *sprigs thyme*
1 *tablespoon Worcestershire sauce*
1 *tablespoon minced celery*
salt and pepper to taste

Melt 3 tablespoons lard in a Dutch oven. Wash the tripe and cut it into 1-inch squares, and add it to the hot lard with the cloves. Let steam, covered, until the water from the tripe has been drawn out and the tripe starts frying. Place the onions and garlic in a frying pan with 3 tablespoons lard, and brown over a low flame. Stir in the flour until it is brown. Place the onions, garlic, and browned flour in the pot with the tripe. Add the tomatoes and all other ingredients. Let cook until tender. Serves 7 to 8.

Savory Kidney Stew

4 *large veal kidneys, or 6 small*   2 *tablespoons parsley*
   kidneys   2 *tablespoons chopped celery*
2 *tablespoons lard*   2 *teaspoons salt*
3 *whole cloves*   ¼ *teaspoon black pepper*
2 *onions, minced fine*   2 *dashes cayenne pepper*
3 *cloves garlic, minced fine*   2 *bay leaves*
1 *tablespoon flour*   1 *sprig thyme*

Cut the fat from the kidneys, then cut them up in small pieces. Melt the lard in a pot and add the kidneys and cloves. Cover the pot and cook until the water has been drawn from the kidneys and they start frying—the loud popping noise when the cover is first put on is the water frying out; when this stops the kidneys are actually beginning to fry. Take the kidneys out of the pot and put in the onions and garlic. Fry until they are brown, stir in the flour, let it brown for 5 minutes, then put the kidneys back in the pot with 1 cup hot water and the rest of the ingredients. Let cook 30 minutes. Serve in individual covered dishes with rice.

Ragout of Squirrel

Muskrats may be substituted for squirrels in this dish. (Jesse says muskrats make better eating than squirrels, but they are hard to obtain.) Be sure to remove the musk sac from the squirrel when cleaning it.

3 *or 4 squirrels*   1 *tablespoon minced celery*
3 *tablespoons oil*   2 *sprigs thyme*
2 *whole cloves*   1 *teaspoon Worcestershire sauce*
2 *onions, minced*   ½ *teaspoon white or black*
3 *cloves garlic, minced*   *pepper*
2 *tablespoons flour*   1 *teaspoon salt (to start)*

Skin and wash the squirrels, and cut them up as you would chickens. Put the oil in a pan, add cloves and squirrels. Simmer until brown, then take the squirrels out of the oil. Brown the onions and garlic in the oil over a low flame, and stir in the flour until brown. Put the squirrels back in the pot, add 1½ cups water and all other ingredients. Cook 1 hour or until tender. Serves 5 or 6.

Possum and Sweet Potatoes

This is a real Deep South country dish, one which few city dwellers or even noted restaurateurs know how to prepare.

First acquire a possum, have it killed and skinned, and have the four musk sacs taken out. This must be done by an experienced possum cook; the musk, if not removed, will cause the meat to taste "strong."

1 *possum (6 to 8 lbs.)*	1 *tablespoon chopped celery*
2 *onions, chopped*	3 *whole cloves*
3 *cloves garlic*	3 *whole allspice*
1 *tablespoon thyme*	2 *tablespoons salt*
3 *bay leaves*	⅛ *teaspoon red pepper*
1 *tablespoon fresh parsley, chopped*	6 *large sweet potatoes, boiled, skinned, and sliced*

Put the possum to boil in a pot of water containing all ingredients except the sweet potatoes. Boil for 2½ to 3 hours. When the possum is tender, take it out and place it in a baking pan. Surround it with the sliced sweet potatoes. Brown the possum and potatoes on both sides in a 350° oven. A 6- to 8-pound possum will serve 6 or 7 people.

A raccoon may be prepared in the same manner.

Ragout of Diamond-Back Terrapin

Diamond-back terrapin is one of the costliest of restaurant dishes and the hardest to find, even in Louisiana, where the little turtles inhabit marshes, bayous, and swamps, and sometimes may be seen in the light from a car as they attempt to cross a highway. Once quite common in New Orleans' famous French Market, the lordly terrapin, prepared in a ragout or stew, can now be encountered only on the most expensive menus.

H. L. Mencken, who worked as a newspaperman with my father in Baltimore at the turn of the century, and was a frequent visitor at our home in Bay St. Louis, Mississippi, in the 1920s and early 1930s, regarded Jesse's Ragout of Diamond-Back Terrapin as one of his favorite dishes, and Mother always arranged to serve it at least once on his visits. Whenever Jesse begins to prepare this dish he thinks of the time many years ago when Samuel Zemurray, managing director of the United Fruit Company, borrowed him to prepare a terrapin ragout for a stag dinner. What keeps the incident particularly green in Jesse's memory is the fact that he got twenty-two dollars in cash and a set of new tires for his jalopy, for preparing, cooking, and serving this delectable dish.

If you can corral some diamond-back terrapin and really want to impress your guests, here is how to prepare and cook the terrapin.

4 "count-size" terrapin (about 2½ lbs. each)
3 tablespoons lard
2 large onions, chopped fine
4 cloves garlic, minced
3 tablespoons flour
2 bay leaves
1 sprig thyme
2 whole cloves
2 tablespoons cut-up parsley
2 tablespoons cut-up celery
2 dashes cayenne or red pepper
1 teaspoon salt (to start)
½ teaspoon black pepper
1 tablespoon Worcestershire sauce
2 tablespoons fresh lemon juice
½ cup sherry

The most difficult part of the proceedings, in my opinion, is killing the terrapins. Jesse forces their heads out of their shells with a sharp stick, then cuts the heads off with a cleaver. He hangs the turtles up, neck down, and lets the blood drain into a pan or the sink for 10 minutes.

The next step is to remove the meat from the turtle's armor shell. To do this, set a dishpan of water on the stove and let the water come to a boil. Drop the whole turtle into the water and let it remain for 5 minutes. Remove from the water, let cool, and then cut the chest plate off with a sharp knife. Carve out the turtle meat and cut off the feet. Put the meat and feet back in the hot water for a few minutes to loosen the tough skin. Cut up the meat into squares, and cut the skin off the feet, leaving the legs whole. You are now ready to prepare the ragout proper.

Place the lard in a Dutch oven or aluminum pot, melt it, and add the turtle meat. Let the meat steam, covered, for 20 minutes, until it is tender and brown. Take the meat out, place it on a platter, add the onions and garlic to the lard, and let simmer until they are brown, stirring constantly. When the vegetables are brown, add the flour. Stir until the flour is brown, and put the meat back into the pot. Add 2½ cups cold water, the bay leaves, thyme, cloves, parsley, celery, pepper, and salt, and let simmer until the stew thickens—about 1½ hours.

Just before serving, add the Worcestershire sauce, lemon juice, and sherry. Serve the ragout in individual casseroles, accompanied by rice, broccoli, green peas, and a tossed salad. Serves 6.

Roast Wild Duck

Louisiana, with its thousands of square miles of lakes and bayous, is great duck country, and roast wild duck forms a part of the native cuisine in the wintertime. As it is illegal to sell wild ducks, you must either shoot them yourself or depend on the bounty of your duck-hunting friends for the *pièce de résistance* of this regal dish. This recipe is suitable for either the wild or tame variety of duck. Three small ducks will serve 6; one large duck serves 4. Jesse serves this with broiled fruit (page 130).

3 *small ducks, or* 1 *large duck*
salt and pepper

STUFFING
7½ *tablespoons lard*
4 *onions, minced*
4 *cloves garlic, minced*
½ *pt. fresh oysters with their liquor*
8 *slices bread, toasted*
1½ *teaspoons salt*
1 *teaspoon black pepper*
4 *bay leaves*

4 *sprigs thyme*
2 *tablespoons minced parsley*
2 *tablespoons minced celery*
1½ *tablespoons flour*

GRAVY
2 *onions, minced*
3 *cloves garlic, minced*
2 *bay leaves, mashed*
2 *sprigs thyme, mashed*
2 *tablespoons minced parsley*
2 *tablespoons minced celery*
1½ *tablespoons flour*

Pick and clean the ducks, wash them inside and out, and salt and pepper them inside and out.

Make the stuffing as follows: Put the lard to melt in a frying pan, add the onions and garlic, and let them brown. Put the oysters in another pan and let them cook until the edges curl. Strain the liquor out and save it; cut up the oysters into fine pieces. Put the oysters in the pan with the onions and garlic, stirring well. Dampen the toast slices, mash them, and add to the pan with all seasonings, parsley, and celery. Let the mixture cook until it is dried out. Stuff the ducks, sew them up, and grease them outside. Sprinkle them with flour and place in a baking pan.

Pour into the pan 3 cups liquid—the oyster liquor plus water —add the gravy ingredients, and bake in a 350° oven 1 to 2 hours or until the duck is tender.

Wild Duck and Jerusalem Artichokes

The Jerusalem artichokes help absorb any fishy flavor from the duck. If you can't get Jerusalem artichokes, turnips are a good substitute.

4 *small wild ducks*	2 *whole cloves*
salt and pepper	2 *sprigs thyme*
4½ *tablespoons lard*	¼ *teaspoon black pepper*
2 *large onions, minced*	2 *bay leaves*
3 *cloves garlic, chopped very fine*	3 *whole allspice*
7½ *tablespoons flour*	1 *teaspoon salt (to start)*
1 *tablespoon minced celery*	6 *Jerusalem artichokes*
1 *tablespoon minced parsley*	2 *tablespoons sherry*

Pick the ducks and clean them inside and out. Salt and pepper them inside and out and sprinkle with flour. Melt the lard in a pot and add the ducks. Let them brown on both sides. Take the ducks out of the pot and brown the onions and garlic in the lard. Stir in the flour and brown it. Put the ducks, celery, parsley, and all seasonings in the pot, add 1½ cups water, and cook 30 minutes. Peel and quarter the Jerusalem artichokes, add them, and cook until they are tender. Just before serving, pour in the sherry. Serves 6 to 7.

Leftover-Meat Hash

This dish is ideal as a quick main course. Leftover beef, veal, lamb, ham, or pork may be used.

3 *tablespoons lard*
1 *large onion, minced*
2 *cloves garlic, minced*
1 *tablespoon flour*
2 *cups minced leftover meat*
2 *large potatoes, boiled and diced*

1 *tablespoon chopped celery*
½ *teaspoon salt*
⅛ *teaspoon black or white pepper*
1 *tablespoon parsley, minced*
2 *bay leaves, chopped fine*
1 *sprig thyme*

Melt the lard in a pan, add the onion and garlic, fry until brown. Stir in the flour until it is brown, add the meat and diced potatoes. Add all other ingredients and ½ cup cold water. Cook, stirring to keep the hash from sticking to the pan, until the mixture is dry. The hash is now ready to serve. Serve with boiled or fried hominy. Serves 4 to 5.

Meat Cutlets

This is an excellent, economical way of using leftover meat. Pork, veal, or lamb may be used in this dish. The recipe makes about 16 cutlets.

½ *lb. butter or oleomargarine*
½ *cup flour*
1 *cup light cream*
1 *to 2 lbs. leftover meat*
½ *teaspoon French mustard*
2 *eggs*

dash of cayenne pepper
½ *teaspoon salt*
pepper
1 *teaspoon Worcestershire sauce*
cracker crumbs
fat for frying

Melt the butter or margarine in a pot, add the flour, and stir until smooth. Add the cream, stir until thick, then add ½ cup water and stir again until thick. Chop up the meat and add to the mixture, stirring well; then add the mustard. Beat one egg well, and add it, the cayenne, salt, pepper, and Worcestershire sauce, stirring until thick. Transfer to a platter and place in the refrigerator. When the mixture has hardened (in 15 or 20 minutes), cut it in oblong slices or cubes. Beat an egg and dip the slices in it, then roll them in cracker crumbs and fry them in deep fat until golden brown.

Brown Butcher Sauce

Although this sauce is called a "butcher sauce," one of its functions is to defeat the high price of meat by stretching pork or veal chops and at the same time making even indifferent meat taste delicious.

3 tablespoons lard	1 teaspoon Creole or French
1 large onion, minced	mustard
2 teaspoons flour	2 tablespoons sweet pickles, cut
1 can clear consommé	up small
1½ cups sherry	1 teaspoon pickle liquor

Melt the lard in a saucepan, add the onion, and fry slowly for 10 minutes or until the onion is brown. Add flour, stir for 5 minutes, then pour in the consommé. Let boil 10 minutes. Add the sherry and simmer 30 to 40 minutes. Just before serving, add the mustard and pickles. Pour over chops and serve. Serves 6.

❧ 6 ❧

VEGETABLES

Artichokes with Red-Wine Sauce

The artichoke is the king of New Orleans and Gulf Coast vegetables. It is common in New Orleans and throughout Louisiana, where it is sold from huckster wagons, open-air vegetable and fruit stands, and almost every corner grocery. Artichokes are simple to prepare and cook, and no matter how often they are served they always evoke pleased comment because of their unusual appearance and their unfolding goodness as they are consumed. They did double duty at our home in Mississippi as a vegetable course and a salad. A good red-wine sauce is vital to the success of this dish.

One large artichoke is sufficient to serve one person, so make your purchase according to the number of guests you are entertaining.

artichokes   2 *tablespoons salt*
6 *cloves garlic, sliced*

Prepare each artichoke by holding it by its stem, top side down, and pounding it on a table or drainboard until the leaves open and the artichoke can be washed thoroughly. The pounding and loosening of the leaves not only aids the washing operation but also enables the flavoring to penetrate the innermost leaves and heart during the cooking process.

When the artichoke is washed, mold the leaves back into shape. Cut the stems off the artichokes and place them upright in the pot with the tops of the leaves up. Use a pot that will hold the artichokes firmly side by side without their tipping over. Add

114

cold water to a little more than half of the height of the artichokes. Six cups of water in a medium-sized pot will usually accommodate 4 artichokes.

Add the garlic and the salt to the water. Boil until the leaves of the artichokes will pull off easily with a slight jerk. Drain the water off the artichokes and let them cool. Serve whole on large salad plates (to take care of leaves and discarded portions) with sauce either on the plate or at the side.

To eat an artichoke, pull off the leaves singly, dip the soft, edible end in the sauce, place the end in your mouth, and scrape it between the teeth. After the leaves have been eaten in this fashion, the heart will remain, protected by a soft, rather tasteless skin, with a hairy "choke" underneath. Remove the skin and choke with a knife and discard. Cut up the heart into pieces, and dunk them in the sauce.

RED-WINE SAUCE

This amount will serve 4 persons.

1 *clove garlic*
1 *tablespoon sugar*
1 *teaspoon salt*
dash of black pepper
½ *teaspoon dry mustard*

dash of paprika
4 *oz. salad oil or olive oil*
4 *oz. Burgundy*
1 *tablespoon mayonnaise*

Cut the garlic in half, place it in a small mixing bowl, add sugar, salt, pepper, mustard, and paprika. Mix thoroughly, add the oil, mix, add the wine, mix thoroughly, and stir in the mayonnaise. Serve in individual cups or glasses in equal portions.

Stuffed Artichokes

6 *large artichokes*
3 *slices bacon*
6 *cloves garlic, chopped fine*
½ *cup grated Parmesan cheese*
2 *anchovies, mashed*

1 *tablespoon parsley, chopped fine*
½ *cup breadcrumbs*
1 *teaspoon olive oil (optional)*

Prepare each artichoke for stuffing by holding it by its stalk and pounding it, leaves down, on a drainboard or table until the leaves open. Wash well. Cut off the stems.

Prepare the dressing as follows: Cook 3 slices bacon till crisp, and chop them fine or mash them into tiny crumbs with a fork. In the bacon fat, brown the garlic to a golden color. Add the bacon, grated Parmesan cheese, mashed anchovies, and parsley, and blend thoroughly into a paste or stuffing. Add the breadcrumbs to hold the stuffing together. Moisten, if necessary, with 1 teaspoon olive oil. Stuff small bits of the dressing as far down as possible behind each leaf of the artichokes, and then draw the leaves as tightly together as you can. Stand the artichokes in a pot small enough to wedge them tightly together, so that they will not topple over and so that the dressing cannot escape as they cook. Add enough water to come about one-quarter of the way up on the artichokes, cover the pot, and allow them to boil until done—which is the point at which a leaf may be easily pulled out (about 1 hour of slow boiling is usually long enough if the artichokes are not too old and are fresh and tender). A bit of olive oil and halved cloves of garlic added to the boiling water will greatly improve the flavor. The artichokes should be eaten leaf by leaf, and a tasty mite of the sharp and piquant dressing can be nibbled from the end of each leaf.

Artichokes prepared in this manner are served as a vegetable or appetizer course; but they are also frequently used by the Creoles as a Sunday-night snack or luncheon dainty.

Fresh Asparagus with Goldenrod Sauce

1 *bunch asparagus*   1 *cup medium thick white sauce,*
2 *eggs, hard-boiled and separated*   *well seasoned*

Clean and cook the asparagus, using a large flat pan. Boil until tender, about 12 to 15 minutes. Chop the egg whites fine and add them to the white sauce. Press the yolks through a fine sieve. Place the asparagus on a large hot platter, cover it with the white sauce, and sprinkle with the pulverized yolks. Serves 4.

Baked Avocados

Hot avocado dishes are another innovation at our dinnertable since my own sojourn in South Florida, where, in Miami and Key West, I found these hitherto salad-only favorites baked with meats and shellfish into myriads of delicious confections. Diced baked ham or chicken or a mixture of the two, boiled shrimp or crabmeat, fresh or canned fish, are the favorite fillings when South Floridians (or their Cuban neighbors, who probably originated the idea) stuff avocados to bake them. Miamians and Key Westers merely make a thick white sauce, add salt and pepper and the chosen stuffing material, and fill the hollows of halved avocados. The avocados may be peeled or not. Most Miamians and Key Westers then simply sprinkle the top with cheese (usually of the sharp American or Cheddar variety) and bake for about 15 minutes at 375° or until the cheese is slightly browned. They say that if you wish to put a few drops of garlic vinegar on the avocado before baking, it will improve the flavor.

They also sometimes grease a baking dish and alternate layers of creamed chicken, meat, fish, or shellfish with layers of peeled sliced avocados, ending with a layer of the fish, flesh, or fowl on top. Then they sprinkle on the grated cheese and bake.

Baked Avocados in Ramekins
with Shrimp or Crab

The queen of all hot avocado dishes we've ever encountered, and a favorite for party occasions, is not from Miami, where I encountered so many variations on the avocado theme, but from the distinguished cuisine of Corinne Dunbar's Tearoom in New Orleans. We are justly proud to include in Jesse's book two mainstays of his repertoire which came from this delightful establishment. (For Corinne Dunbar's filling of Vol-au-Vent of Chicken, see page 59.) By special permission of Mrs. Catherine Dunbar Brown, daughter of the restaurant's founder, we publish for the first time the following closely guarded recipe.

5 *lbs. raw, unshelled shrimp, or*
  3 lbs. boiled crabmeat (about 3
  doz. boiled crabs)
1 *lb. butter or half-and-half but-*
  ter and margarine
6 *cans cream of mushroom soup*
1 *can evaporated milk, or same*
  amount of milk and cream

salt and pepper to taste
8 *fairly large and firm but well-*
  ripened avocados, peeled and
  diced
breadcrumbs
1 *can fillets of anchovies*
1 *small can pimiento*

First, a word about the shrimp or crabs you use. The shrimp should be shelled and boiled properly, and the more attention you give this process, the better the final result will be (see Jesse's recipe, page 3). Also, we must emphasize that if you use crabmeat it should be either fresh-boiled or of the fresh-boiled variety sold in cans, iced but *not* frozen. This product is sold at all Coast seaports and is regularly shipped, packed in ice, from Coast towns to virtually all points in the country, and is re-iced en route. Crabmeat that has been frozen is unsuitable for this or any other use, in our opinion.

Now for the preparation of the dish: Melt all the butter and margarine (if you use it), except for a small piece, which you should leave in the refrigerator to keep it firm. Add mushroom soup to the melted butter, and then add the shrimp or crabmeat, stirring to keep smooth and prevent lumping or browning on the bottom. Let simmer for 10 to 15 minutes. Stir in the evaporated milk or milk-cream mixture. Add salt and pepper to taste; if the shrimp or crab has been well flavored in boiling, about ½ teaspoon salt and several generous dashes of black or white pepper should be a good starter. Stir and simmer 5 or 10 minutes more until the mixture is smooth and thick. Place a layer of diced avocado in the bottoms of ramekins, and then pour in a layer of sauce. Repeat this procedure until the ramekins have been filled to the desired proportions. Sprinkle the tops with breadcrumbs, or crumbs made from crisp toast slices. Dot with bits of butter and place a fillet of anchovy atop each ramekin. Dribble a few drops of the anchovy oil over each ramekin, and garnish with bright pimiento strips or cubes. Pop the ramekins into a 375° to 400° oven just long enough to get the whole mixture heated well and the cream sauce bubbly. Serve at once. The degree to which you fill your ramekins will have some bearing on the number of portions this will make, but with average-sized ramekins, filled three-quarters full, this recipe should afford 10 to 12 servings.

Baked Bananas

This is one of Jesse's most delectable dishes. Easy to prepare, it always hits the spot with dinner guests. This recipe will serve 6.

12 *small or 6 large, firm, ripe bananas*
¼ *lb. butter or oleomargarine*

½ *cup granulated sugar*
2 *tablespoons powdered cinnamon*

Peel the bananas and place them, whole, in rows in a baking pan. Cut the butter or oleomargarine in ¼-inch squares and distribute it over the bananas. Sprinkle with sugar, then cinnamon. Add 2 cups cold water to the pan, place in a 350° oven, and bake for 1 hour. Baste every 20 minutes, but don't turn or disturb the bananas. Serve in an open dish as a vegetable course.

Red Beans and Rice Peckerwood

This famous Southern dish will really stick to your ribs. Jesse has improved on the standard "peckerwood" (backwoods) recipe by adding a dash of Creole flavoring.

1 *lb. red kidney beans*
1 *lb. cured ham or slab bacon (lean)*
2 *large onions, chopped fine*
3 *cloves garlic, chopped fine*
3 *bay leaves*

1 *tablespoon chopped celery*
1 *tablespoon fresh parsley, chopped fine*
salt and pepper to taste
3 *cups cooked rice (page 138)*

Soak the beans 20 or 30 minutes, pour off the water, and cover with fresh water 4 inches over the beans. Add the meat in one piece, onions, garlic, bay leaves, celery, and parsley, and boil until creamy, about 1½ hours. Add salt and pepper to taste if necessary. Serve with the rice, putting some of the beans and their rich sauce over the rice. Serves 4 to 5.

Smothered Snap Beans

This is a fine side dish which can be served with almost any meat.

2 *lbs. fresh, or 2 cans, snap beans* ½ *teaspoon salt*
1½ *lbs. slab bacon or cured ham* 1 *tablespoon bacon grease, drip-*
1 *large onion, chopped fine* *pings, or lard*

Prepare fresh beans by snapping off the ends and cutting up the beans. Put the bacon or ham and the onion in a pot with 2 cups water, let boil 15 minutes, add the beans, boil 15 minutes longer, then add ½ teaspoon salt and 1 tablespoon bacon grease, drippings, or lard. Cook young tender beans 30 minutes longer, older ones 40 minutes. Canned beans may be done in 10 minutes. Serves 5 to 6.

New Beets with Orange Sauce

8 *new beets, or 1 large can beets* 3 *or 4 whole allspice*
3 *teaspoons grated orange rind* ½ *cup orange juice*
6 *tablespoons sugar* 4 *teaspoons butter*
¼ *teaspoon salt* ½ *tablespoon cornstarch dis-*
2 *small pieces stick cinnamon* *solved in 1 teaspoon water*
6 *whole cloves*

Clean the beets and cook them until tender (or heat canned beets). Drain. Cook the grated rind, sugar (the amount will vary according to the sweetness of the orange), salt, cinnamon, cloves, allspice, orange juice, and 1 tablespoon water for 5 minutes. Add the butter to the mixture. Add the dissolved cornstarch and cook slowly until the mixture is thick. Strain. Pour over the beets.

Canned beets are wonderful when prepared in this way, and beet liquor may be substituted for the water. Jesse likes the sauce about the consistency of fresh light cream. If your hand slips on the cornstarch, add orange juice and beet juice. Serves 4.

Sunday-Dinner Broccoli

Broccoli is usually served buried under a thick cream sauce. Jesse serves it with a Drawn Butter Sauce so as not to obscure the distinctive flavor of the tender stalks and flowers.

2 *bunches broccoli*   1 *teaspoon baking soda*
salt and pepper to taste

Since the stalks of broccoli are less tender than the flowers, they should be cooked longer. A simple method is to wash the broccoli thoroughly, then tie the stalks together with white string and stand the broccoli upright in a deep pot. Add 1 teaspoon salt, 1 teaspoon baking soda, and water two-thirds of the way up the stalks. Let the water come to a full boil, then pour the water off and add 1 cup fresh water. Cover and steam for 15 minutes, or until the stalks are tender. The soda will impart a fresh green look to the broccoli. Salt and pepper to taste. Serve with Drawn Butter Sauce or Hollandaise Sauce.

DRAWN BUTTER SAUCE

¼ *lb. butter*   ⅓ *lemon*

Melt the butter in a saucepan, shaking the pan over a low flame until all the water has left the butter. You will know this has happened when the bubbling butter ceases to crackle or hiss but continues to bubble silently and begins to turn brown. At this strategic moment "draw" the butter by squeezing about ⅓ of a lemon into it and dropping the rind in. The butter will foam or froth and then settle with a rich brown thickness at the bottom. Always serve the sauce hot, over broiled or boiled fish, omelets, broiled lamb chops, broccoli, or other vegetables.

HOLLANDAISE SAUCE

¼ cup butter

2 egg yolks

½ tablespoon lemon juice

generous pinch of salt

dash of cayenne pepper

dash of nutmeg

Cream the butter and add the egg yolks to it, one by one. Place in a double boiler over very hot but not boiling water, and cook until the mixture begins to thicken. Add the lemon juice, salt, pepper, and nutmeg. Stir until thick, then add slowly ½ cup boiling water—slowly, slowly, as in making mayonnaise, and you won't need to worry about the eggs' curdling. Keep stirring until the sauce is like thick cream or mayonnaise. This is delicious over vegetables such as spinach, broccoli, and asparagus, or over almost any kind of fish.

Brussels Sprouts

Brussels Sprouts are first cousins to cabbage, and, like cabbage, must be well seasoned to bring out their full attractiveness as a vegetable.

2 boxes fresh or frozen Brussels
  sprouts

½ teaspoon baking soda

salt and pepper to taste

If Brussels Sprouts are fresh, clean and wash them. Put the sprouts in a pot with a small amount of water and the baking soda. Let come to a quick boil. Remove from the fire, pour into a colander, and wash the soda out. Put back in a pot with fresh water. Put on a slow fire and cook for 15 to 20 minutes. Salt and pepper to taste. Serve with a butter sauce or a white cream sauce. Serves 5 to 6.

Boiled Cabbage

1 *3-lb. cabbage*	½ *teaspoon pepper*
1 *teaspoon salt*	*melted butter*

Wash a 3-pound cabbage, remove the hard core, and cut the cabbage in quarters. Put in a pot with 1 quart water, 1 teaspoon salt, and ½ teaspoon pepper. Let boil for 15 minutes. Serve with melted butter. Serves 4 to 5.

Smothered Cabbage

Excellent with baked or roasted fresh ham.

3 *tablespoons fat*	1 *3-lb. cabbage*
1 *lb. sliced cured ham*	*salt and pepper*
1 *large onion, minced*	

Melt the fat. Place the ham in the fat and let it fry until brown. Add the minced onion and stir well for 5 minutes. Wash the cabbage and cut it in thin slices. Put in the pot with the ham and add ½ cup cold water. Salt and pepper to taste. Cover and let cook 20 minutes. Serves 4 to 5.

Steamed Cabbage

1 *3-lb. cabbage*	*melted butter*
4 *slices bacon*	*salt and pepper*

Remove the hard core from a 3-pound cabbage. Cut the cabbage in quarters. Wrap a slice of bacon around each quarter and place in a colander. Place the colander over a large pot so that the cabbage can steam. Put 1 quart water in the pot and steam for 30 minutes. Pour melted butter over the cabbage, salt and pepper, and serve. Serves 4 to 5.

Cauliflower with Cheese

An aristocratic dish, which goes well with almost any meat course.

1 *large cauliflower or 2 small ones*
4 *tablespoons butter or oleomargarine*

3 *tablespoons flour*
1 *cup milk, heated but not boiled*
½ *cup grated American cheese*
salt and pepper

Boil the cauliflower until tender. Make a cream sauce as follows:

Put the butter or oleomargarine to melt in a pot, stir in the flour until smooth, then pour the milk in gradually, stirring well. (Canned evaporated milk may be used instead of fresh milk.) Stir the milk in over a low fire until the sauce is thick. Add 2 tablespoons grated cheese and salt and pepper. Cover the bottom of a Pyrex dish with grated cheese, take the cauliflower apart and arrange the flowerets in the dish, then cover with sauce and sprinkle liberally with remaining grated cheese. Bake in a 350° oven until cheese is lightly browned on top.

Corn Pudding

For a delicious vegetable dish that will complement almost any kind of meal and that looks and tastes like a million dollars' worth of time and effort but actually takes only minutes to prepare, Jesse's simple corn pudding is tops. It differs from a soufflé in that you don't beat the egg whites so much, and it's not quite as high-rising. But it puffs delightfully just the same, and there's compensation for the lack of rising. You can take it out of the oven when it's done, set it aside on top of the stove, and run it back into the oven for a few minutes just before serving, without losing flavor or consistency. (Any devotee of soufflés knows what dismal results would occur if you didn't pop the soufflé right on the table directly from the oven.) Corn pudding is not only a tasty dish but downright nourishing, and most babies and small children consume it with relish.

1 *slice bacon*	4 *to 8 tablespoons sugar*
1 *can cream-style corn*	*pinch of salt*
2 *eggs* (1 *whole*, 1 *separated*)	1 *cup milk*

Cut a slice of bacon into about four pieces and fry until about three-quarters done (so it is not too crisp). Pour the fat into a pie pan, glass baking dish, or any utensil in which you wish to bake the pudding. Grease the dish well and then pour off the excess fat.

Pour the corn into the dish (Jesse prefers yellow corn, but you can use the white kind too), add the milk, and stir in (do *not* beat!) one whole egg and the yolk of another. Break up the egg well all through the corn—this can best be done with an ordinary table fork. Sprinkle in, while stirring, 4 to 8 tablespoons sugar, according to the dictates of your own sweet tooth. The original sweetness of the corn, plus individual taste, rules the sugar quota, so suppose you start with 4 heaping tablespoons in the first pudding and work up or down from there.

Add a pinch of salt and stir in well, and then beat the white remaining from the second egg and fold it in. Before putting this in the oven, slip little bits of bacon around the edge of the dish. Bake in a 350° to 375° oven 40 minutes, or until the center is firm.

You can mix this pudding in the morning, except for the beaten egg white, and set it in the refrigerator until later, if you allow it to get to room temperature before attempting to bake it, and also give it a twirl with the fork at the last minute to mix everything up well again. Add the beaten egg white at the last minute. For that matter, I have made a very successful corn pudding, if not quite as light a one, by mixing it all beforehand and not even beating the second egg white separately at all. This is really a time-saver for a party or for a big family dinner, as it can be mixed beforehand and cooked along with the roast, and adds greatly to any menu. Serves 4 to 5.

Corn Soufflé

This is a very satisfactory vegetable dish.

4 *tablespoons butter*
2 *egg yolks*
1½ *tablespoons sugar*
1 *can whole-kernel corn*

1 *cup evaporated milk*
½ *teaspoon salt*
2 *egg whites*
dash of pepper

Cream the butter in a mixing bowl, add the egg yolks, and stir until well mixed. Add the sugar, corn, milk, and salt. Beat the whites of the eggs and fold them in. Place the mixture in a Pyrex baking dish and bake in a slow oven (275°) until browned—45 minutes to 1 hour. Serves 5 to 6.

Baked Eggplant with Shrimp or Tuna Fish

If you don't tell your guests beforehand what is in this dish, we'll wager that they'll never be able to guess—average people, that is. Many of our visiting gourmets, who have confessed afterward that they "never touch" either of the main ingredients separately, devour them in this symphony and always come back for more. Distinctive as the flavors of shrimp, tuna fish, and eggplant are, they present an entirely new taste adventure when blended. Dry, golden toast crumbs made in your own oven are a key to the success of the dish, not only for binding the ingredients and flavors, but for giving the dish a light fluffiness instead of a soggy, heavy base.

5 *slices bread*
1 *large eggplant or 2 small ones*
1 *heaping tablespoon salt*
1 *lb. headless shrimp, or 1½ lbs. shrimp with the heads on (or 1 large can tuna fish)*
2 *medium-sized onions, minced*
bacon fat
butter or oleomargarine
2 *bay leaves*
salt and pepper to taste

1 *sprig fresh thyme, or pinch of canned thyme leaves (not powdered thyme)*
dash of Tabasco Sauce
¾ *cup evaporated milk*
1 *can strained chicken broth (with tuna fish)*
¼ *lb. American-type cheese, grated*
5 *or 6 oz. sherry*

Toast the bread, then place it in a slow oven until the slices have dried out and become brown and light. Roll them with a rolling pin, or tie them in a cloth and mash with a mallet.

Peel the eggplant and cut it into slices and then into small cubes about the size of marbles. Put these to soak in a brine solution made with 1 heaping tablespoon salt and 2 quarts water, in a large mixing bowl. The eggplant will float, so weigh it down with a lid or inverted plate to get it well soaked. After about ½ to ¾ hour pour off the salt water (you will see that the liquid is brown; it has drawn much of the "bite" out of the eggplant), and let the eggplant soak in plain water until you are ready to use it.

Clean the shrimp by removing the shells and the veins from the backs, and put the shells on to simmer in water enough to cover. Brown the onions slowly in bacon fat and a small bit of butter or margarine, until they are soft and golden. Add bay leaves, salt, pepper, thyme, and a dash or so of Tabasco Sauce or other hot seasoning. Drain the eggplant well to get as much of the water off as possible, add to the onions, and fry it down until it is soft, slightly browned, and about half its original volume (it shrinks quickly). Add the shrimp and stir until the shrimp have fried slightly. Add most of the toast crumbs, the evaporated milk, and at least ½ cup liquid from the pot in which the shells have been simmering. Add the grated cheese. Salt and pepper to taste, then add the sherry. Stir over a low flame until the mixture has thickened but is still soft enough to allow for baking. Sprinkle crumbs over the top and bake in a 350° oven until bubbly and brown on top.

If you wish to substitute tuna fish for the shrimp, the dish will be just as delicious if you add a can of strained chicken broth to the mixture in place of the moisture from the shrimp-shell water. This will fill a large baking dish and will provide for 4 to 6 persons generously when served as a vegetable with either meat or fish.

Broiled Citrus Fruits and Apples

Bright grilled citrus fruits add color, sparkle, and flavor to a number of Jesse's masterpieces. His roast duck, for instance, beautifully browned, is served on a large platter, garnished with lettuce leaves, parsley bunches, and grilled grapefruit topped with oranges, baked apples, and grilled tomatoes.

To prepare the grapefruit (½ grapefruit for each serving), Jesse slices the fruit in half and scallops the edges. He loosens the segments with a knife, as if for breakfast serving, and spreads sugar liberally over the top. He then places peeled orange segments, cartwheel fashion, atop the grapefruit halves, and tops off each orange wheel with a plump maraschino cherry. Cognac, brandy, or rum is poured generously over all, and the whole thing is sprinkled with a bit more sugar before it is popped into the broiler for browning just before serving on the platter around the duck. Apples (one to a serving), peeled halfway down, are put under the broiler for a few seconds to soften the pulp, and then splashed with rum or whisky, sprinkled with a mixture of sugar and cinnamon, decorated with cherry segments cartwheeled on top, and given a final browning. They are placed alternately with grapefruit halves around the roast duck or other poultry.

Boiled Okra

One of the most maligned and yet one of the most unusual of all Southern vegetables is okra. Here's Jesse's way of cooking it so that it does not become slimy or "seedy." One pound will serve 4 to 5.

First, be sure to get young, tender okra. You can tell this usually by the size. Reject long, hard, ridged specimens and choose small, round, plump ones. Cut off the stems, put in water

(3 cups water to 1 dozen okra) with a dash of baking soda, and boil 20 minutes. Place in a colander and run cold water over the okra to eliminate any slime. Keep warm in the colander over hot water until ready to serve. Pour melted butter over the okra and serve with salt and pepper to taste.

Okra Succotash

This is an exotic side dish that everyone will like. Be sure to use fresh or frozen okra. Do not attempt this recipe with the canned product.

3 tablespoons lard or fat
1 lb. fresh or frozen okra, cut up
2 onions, chopped fine
3 cloves garlic, minced
½ lb. ham, diced
1 No. 2 can tomatoes or 4 fresh skinned tomatoes
1 can butterbeans or 1 cup cooked fresh butterbeans

1 can corn kernels
1 tablespoon minced parsley
1 tablespoon minced celery
1 bay leaf, mashed
1 sprig thyme, shredded
4 tablespoons butter or oleomargarine
½ teaspoon sugar
salt and pepper to taste

Melt the lard in a heavy aluminum pot, add the cut-up okra, and fry until the okra is not ropy. Add the onions and garlic, fry 5 minutes. Add the ham and tomatoes and fry 5 minutes. Add all other ingredients and cook 20 to 30 minutes over a medium flame. Serves 5 to 6.

Stuffed Sweet Peppers

Use large, crisp sweet peppers for this dish.

6 *sweet peppers*

3 *tablespoons lard or fat*

2 *onions, minced*

3 *cloves garlic, minced*

½ *lb. shrimp, shelled and cleaned*

1 *teaspoon minced celery*

½ *teaspoon black pepper*

1 *bay leaf*

1 *sprig thyme, shredded*

1 *teaspoon Worcestershire sauce*

1 *teaspoon salt*

8 *slices toast*

1 *egg*

breadcrumbs

butter

Put the peppers in hot water for 3 minutes to make them firm. Take them out and let them cool. Cut the peppers in halves from top to bottom, clean out the seeds, and trim the inside ridges. Chop up the seeds and trimmings fine. Melt the lard in a frying pan, add the onions and garlic, cook until brown. Add the pepper seeds and trimmings. Cut the shrimp fine, place in the pot with the onions and garlic. Add celery and all seasonings, cook for 10 minutes. Moisten the toast, mix it in well with onion-and-shrimp mixture, stir in the egg, and cook for 5 minutes. Stuff into the pepper halves and lay them flat in a pan. Sprinkle with breadcrumbs, dot with butter, and bake 15 to 20 minutes in a 450° oven. Serves 6 to 7.

Southern French-Fried Potatoes

6 *large potatoes*   *fat*

Peel the potatoes, put them in a pot, cover them with water, and let boil until almost done. Cool and slice the potatoes in longish strips, then place them in the refrigerator for 15 minutes. Remove, dry, and fry in deep fat. Serves 4 to 5.

Baked Sweet Potatoes Marshmallow

This is a showy and delicious vegetable dish and a great favorite at our table. You may substitute pumpkin or cushaw for the sweet potatoes.

4 *large or 8 small sweet potatoes*	1½ *tablespoons sugar*
1½ *cups sweet milk*	2 *teaspoons cinnamon*
¼ *lb. butter*	2 *eggs, well beaten*
pinch of salt	1 *package marshmallows*

Boil the potatoes until soft, let them cool, peel them, and mash them in a bowl. Add milk, butter, salt, and sugar, stirring until fluffy. Add cinnamon and eggs. Mix well, place in a large Pyrex dish, and bake in a 350° oven until brown. Take out, cover with marshmallows, and brown quickly in the broiler. If you haven't a very large baking dish, you may have to use two smaller ones. Serves 7 to 8.

Candied Yams

One of the most popular of all Southern vegetable dishes.

6 *large yams*	*cinnamon*
1 *cup granulated sugar*	¼ *lb. butter*

Boil 6 large yams, let cool, peel and slice them. Place in a baking pan. Distribute 1 cup of sugar over them and sift cinnamon over them. Put small pieces of butter here and there over the top and add 1 pint water. Bake in a 350° oven until brown—40 to 50 minutes. The water, sugar, and butter will form a thick sirup for the potatoes. Serves 6 to 8.

Sweet-Potato–Apple Bake

Jesse insists this recipe is original and was actually born of neces-
sity when the arrival of unexpected guests once forced him to
invent a dish that has proved to be one of his favorite culinary
successes. Having only three large yams on hand and not much
of any other vegetable to substitute on the menu when the extra
visitors showed up, Jesse racked his brain to decide how he could
stretch the scant potato supply into anything like enough for
serving baked potatoes as he had planned. An idea was born
when he spied three tart and shiny cooking apples winking from
the refrigerator shelf! This recipe serves 4 to 6.

3 *large yams*	*butter*
3 *tart cooking apples*	*cinnamon*
several tablespoons dark brown	*nutmeg*
sugar	*orange marmalade*
pinch of salt	*granulated white sugar*

He simply boiled the yams until they were about half done—
to put them on a par with the apples as to baking time—and
sliced one of them into a baking dish. Over the slices he sprinkled
liberally several tablespoonfuls of dark brown sugar, plus a little
salt, dotted this with bits of butter, added a generous dusting of
cinnamon and nutmeg, and—of all things!—a few dabs of orange
marmalade (the kind with the peelings left in the preserve). Next
came a layer of sliced apples with the same brown-sugar-butter-
spice-and-marmalade garnish. Then he added another layer of
garnished yam slices, and so on, ending with a flourish by jauntily
cartwheeling thick quarter-slices of apple in two neat rings on
top for the final touch of splendor. More sugar, more butter,
more spices, more dabs of marmalade were added, and even a
sprinkling of granulated white sugar over the brown for a glis-
tening finish. That night the new dish made its successful debut
with nary an "FGS" (family go slow) order from my mother, so

little did the apples shrink and so well did they bolster the ample baked-yam casserole. And although we were enthusiastic in our praises, it was months before Jesse admitted that he hadn't known about the combination all along!

I have since heard about such a combination, called Sweet Potato Compote, and Jesse has himself experimented with variations on the formula, adding nuts or raisins, and even topping the dish with marshmallows, which he browns just before sending to the table. But I still think his original bake is just as delicious as any more elaborate version.

Baked Pumpkin

1 5-*lb. pumpkin*	2 *eggs, well beaten*
¼ *lb. butter*	1½ *cups sweet milk*
2 *cups sugar*	2 *teaspoons cinnamon*

Peel the pumpkin and cut it up in small pieces. Boil in 1 cup water until creamy (about 1 to 1½ hours, depending on the size and age of the pumpkin). Add butter, sugar, eggs, milk, and cinnamon. Whip well and bake in a Pyrex bowl or pie pan in a 350° oven until brown. Serves 6.

Baked Cushaw (Crooked-Neck Pumpkin)

The cushaw is a large pumpkin much prized by the Creoles. Skin a 5-pound cushaw, cut it open, remove seeds and pulp. Taste the pulp; if it is bitter, don't bother to cook the cushaw, as it will be unpalatable. If it is sweet, cut up the flesh in 2-inch cubes, place in a pot with 2 cups water and 1 cup sugar, and let boil until creamy—about 1 hour. Take off the stove. Stir in ½ cup sugar, 1 teaspoon cinnamon, ¼ pound butter, and 1 beaten egg. Place the mixture in a Pyrex bowl and bake for 30 minutes in a 300° oven. Cushaw goes well with any type of meat or fish.

Spinach Bouffant

There have been a lot of undeserved jokes about spinach, but the smart hostess should not overlook this dish in planning a dinner. Jesse's Spinach Bouffant on butter-crisped toast is a striking dish to look at and wonderful to eat. Children, traditionally opposed to spinach, devour it with gusto.

2 lbs. fresh spinach or 2 boxes frozen spinach	3 slices toast
	melted butter
½ teaspoon baking soda	½ pt. cream, whipped
1 tablespoon butter	salt (if necessary)
½ cup milk	2 hard-boiled eggs (optional)
salt and pepper	pecans (optional)

If fresh spinach is used, wash it well to get all the grit out, then put it in a pot containing 1 cup water. Add ½ teaspoon baking soda (to keep the spinach green), let come to a quick boil, then take out the spinach and wash out the soda in a colander. (Cook frozen spinach until it is thawed.) Put the spinach in a frying pan with the butter and let simmer 10 minutes. Pour in the milk, salt and pepper to taste, and simmer 15 to 20 minutes longer. Butter-crisp the toast by dicing it, dropping it in hot butter (be sure you have the butter hot and the bread well toasted), and shaking it until crisp. Or remove the crusts and crisp the slices. Right before serving, fold lightly whipped cream into the spinach and arrange on a platter with a wreath of butter-crisped toast dices, or pile individual servings on slices of butter-crisped toast to be served on a platter. If you serve the spinach in a toast ring, place sections of hard-boiled egg and, if desired, halves of pecans, on top. If served on toast slices, the mounds of fluffy green are beautiful either plain or topped with pecan halves. Serves 4 to 5.

Country-Style Turnip Greens

Greens are a true Southern dish, but they must be flavored well in the cooking. Jesse's Country-Style Turnip Greens call for ham, slab bacon, or pork, and an onion.

2 *bunches fresh turnip greens*	1 *tablespoon lard*
½ *lb. ham, bacon, or pork*	*salt and pepper to taste*
1 *medium-sized onion, minced*	*dash of Tabasco Sauce*

Wash the greens four or five times, until all grit is out. Put the meat in a pot with the onion and lard. Let fry 5 minutes, then add 2 cups water and put in the greens. Boil 15 minutes. Add salt and pepper to taste and a dash of Tabasco Sauce.

Fried Grits

These go well with pork sausage.

2 *cups grits*	*evaporated milk* (or 1 *egg*)
1 *teaspoon salt*	*flour*

Boil the grits with salt until they are creamy; set them aside in a large shallow dish or platter. When they are cool and solid, cut them into squares. Dip the squares in evaporated milk, roll them in flour, and fry them in a greased pan. Brown them on both sides. For a thicker batter, beat up an egg, dip the slices in egg, roll them in flour, and fry them in a covered pan. Grits may also be rolled in flour, without the milk or batter, and fried very satisfactorily.

Macaroni and Cheese

1 *lb. macaroni*   2 *dashes white or black pepper*
1 *egg*   *dash of cayenne pepper*
1 *cup fresh milk*   ½ *lb. American cheese*
1 *teaspoon salt*

Boil the macaroni until done, drain, and transfer to a mixing bowl. Add the egg, milk, salt, and pepper, stirring well. Grate the cheese, put some on the bottom of a baking dish, and mix most of the rest through the macaroni. Place the macaroni in the baking dish, sprinkle with cheese, and bake in a 350° oven for 15 minutes or until brown. Serves 5 or 6.

Fluffy Rice

Every cook has his or her own method of cooking rice, a staple food in the South and a basic ingredient of hundreds of dishes. Jesse's system will guarantee you a perfect product every time.

2 *cups uncooked rice*   1 *teaspoon salt*
1 *teaspoon vinegar or fresh
   lemon juice*

Wash the rice, put it in a pan, and add water to 3 inches above the rice. Add the vinegar or lemon juice and salt. Boil rapidly until soft—about 20 minutes. The way to tell whether the rice is done is to take out a single grain with a spoon and mash it between the thumb and forefinger. When the rice mashes so that the hard core can no longer be felt, it is cooked. When it is done, drain it in a colander. Place the colander over a pot of hot water on the stove to keep warm. Serves 5 to 6.

✹ 7 ✹

SALADS

Lettuce-and-Tomato Salad

A lettuce-and-tomato salad goes well with any fish dinner and is compatible with almost any meat. If you want to dress it up, add half a bunch of watercress to this recipe. This will serve 4 to 5.

4 *medium-sized tomatoes*
1 *head crisp lettuce*

Sweet French Dressing (see page 147)

Pull the lettuce leaves apart and spread them on plates. Cut tomatoes in eighths and arrange in equal portions on plates over lettuce leaves. Chill in the refrigerator for ½ hour. Pour Sweet French Dressing over all and serve.

A tossed salad may be made by cutting up tomatoes and lettuce into a large wooden salad bowl. (Etiquette decrees that you should break up the lettuce with the fingers and not cut it with a knife, but we find a knife is cleaner and quicker.) Add sliced ripe olives and a small can of anchovies if desired. Toss well and serve from the bowl at table.

Tossed Salad

1 *large or 2 small cloves garlic, put through garlic press*
½ *head lettuce*
½ *cup salad oil*
1 *anchovy, mashed with a fork and creamed into the oil*
juice of 1 lemon
2 *teaspoons Worcestershire sauce*
½ *teaspoon salt*
pepper to taste
generous pinch of sugar

2 *medium-sized tomatoes*
½ *bell pepper*
½ *bunch watercress*
½ *large or 1 small avocado, peeled and sliced*
4 *stalks celery, chopped (not too fine)*
1 *teaspoon capers*
1 *can large white asparagus tips*
black olives (optional)

If you don't have a garlic press, use ⅛ teaspoon garlic salt, or, well beforehand (for at least 1 hour), marinate 3 cloves garlic cut in large pieces in the oil. Remove the garlic before proceeding with the salad. Break the lettuce into small pieces and marinate it in a mixture of oil, anchovy, lemon juice, 2 teaspoons water, Worcestershire sauce, garlic, salt, pepper, and sugar, until the lettuce has become half wilted—about 10 minutes. Toss the salad vigorously. Just before serving, add the tomatoes, bell pepper, avocado, watercress, celery, and capers. Serve garnished with asparagus tips and black olives. Serves 4 or 5.

Fresh Fruit Salad

2 tart apples, peeled and cubed small

2 small carrots, shaved or grated

½ cup raisins

3 stalks celery, chopped

¼ cup chopped pecans or walnuts

2 eggs

¼ cup sugar

½ cup lemon juice

2 tablespoons white corn sirup

1 teaspoon vinegar

¼ cup half-and-half orange and pineapple juice

All ingredients may be prepared beforehand, except the apples. Peel and cube the apples just before dinner, since they will darken as they stand. Combine the apples, carrots, raisins, celery, and nuts.

Prepare a most unusual dressing by beating the eggs slightly and adding the sugar, lemon juice, sirup, vinegar, and other juices. Place in a double boiler and stir constantly until the mixture begins to thicken. Cool and serve. Spoon the golden-yellow dressing over the salad at table, or mix the fruit and dressing well before serving and top with a very small star of mayonnaise and a whole, half, or section of maraschino cherry on top. Serves 4 to 6.

Honeymoon Salad

From Mrs. Claude Beebe, wife of the president of the Tung Growers Council of America, who resides in DeFuniak Springs, Florida, came the following curious recipe for one of the most delicious salads I have ever tasted. Mrs. Beebe used it on her own honeymoon table, but served it before that too. She says the recipe was given her by an elderly North Florida woman, who said that she had it from her own grandmother. So there's no telling how old the formula really is. But when you try it you won't wonder that it's stood the test of time, nor why it has become one of the stars of Jesse's salad collection. And although you wouldn't think so from reading the directions, this salad is always a prime favorite with men, who invariably ask for more. To make it you'll need:

1 *No. 2 can sliced pineapple*
18 *marshmallows*
1 *cup chopped pecans*
½ *teaspoon salt*
1 *heaping teaspoon flour*
1 *teaspoon dry mustard*

4 *tablespoons thick cream or*
　evaporated milk
1½ *teaspoons butter*
3 *egg yolks*
2 *tablespoons vinegar*
½ *pt. whipping cream*

Cut the sliced pineapple into cubes and dice the marshmallows into small pieces. Combine the pineapple and marshmallows with the chopped pecans.

Make a dressing as follows: Mix thoroughly together the salt, flour, dry mustard, and cream or evaporated milk. Add butter, egg yolks, and vinegar, and mix all thoroughly. Cook this mixture in the top of a double boiler, stirring constantly until it is thick enough to pour from the vessel without sticking.

Pour the hot dressing over pineapple-marshmallow-nut mixture. Set in the refrigerator and chill for 2 or 3 hours or overnight. Whip the cream and fold it into the chilled mixture just before serving. If this has to stand a short while before serving, keep it in the refrigerator.

Cole Slaw

This makes an excellent salad with fried fish and most meats. It is simple and inexpensive, chewy, and aids the digestion of fried or rich foods.

½ *head cabbage, chopped fine*
French Dressing (see page 153)
1 *tablespoon mayonnaise, plus* ½
  teaspoon for garnish

lettuce leaves
¼ *cup grated pecans (optional)*

Chop the cabbage up fine in a salad bowl, pour the French Dressing over the cabbage, add 1 tablespoon mayonnaise, mix well, and place in the refrigerator for ½ hour. Serve on lettuce leaves and garnish with ½ teaspoon mayonnaise just before serving. Addition of the grated nuts adds superb flavor.

Potato Salad

A potato salad, like cabbage dishes, is as good only as its flavoring, and Jesse's version is superb.

2 *lbs. potatoes*
1 *onion*
2 *tablespoons fresh parsley*
2 *tablespoons celery*
1 *tablespoon chopped sweet*
  green pepper
2 *hard-boiled eggs*
1 *clove garlic*

1 *teaspoon Creole or French*
  mustard
6 *tablespoons mayonnaise*
2 *tablespoons vinegar*
2 *tablespoons cooking oil*
1 *tablespoon celery seed*
2 *teaspoons salt*
½ *teaspoon black or white pepper*

Boil the potatoes until soft. Peel, dice, and place in a mixing bowl. Mince the onion, parsley, celery, green pepper, chop up the eggs, and run the garlic through a garlic press or mince it extremely fine. Put all ingredients in with potatoes and mix well; then place in the refrigerator to cool. Serves 6 to 8.

Crab-and-Tomato Salad

A royal salad indeed. This recipe will serve 4 to 6.

1 *lb. fresh crabmeat*
3 *tablespoons mayonnaise*
2 *tablespoons salad oil*
1 *tablespoon vinegar*

½ *teaspoon sugar*
salt and pepper to taste
4 *to 6 medium-sized tomatoes*
1 *head crisp lettuce*

Put the crabmeat in a mixing bowl with mayonnaise, oil, vinegar, and seasoning. Stir without breaking up the crabmeat too much. Hollow out the tomatoes with a sharp knife and fill them with the crabmeat mixture. Arrange on lettuce leaves on salad plates, decorate with sprigs of parsley and a dash of mayonnaise. Serve with crisp crackers.

Shrimp Salad

Jesse serves his shrimp salad on quartered fresh tomatoes and lettuce leaves, with toasted crackers. This recipe will serve 4 to 6.

1 *lb. fresh shrimp, boiled (see pages 3–4)*
1 *teaspoon salad oil*
3 *tablespoons tomato catsup*
salt and pepper to taste
2 *tablespoons mayonnaise*
1 *teaspoon vinegar*

2 *tablespoons chopped sweet green pepper*
½ *teaspoon sugar*
dash of celery seed
1 *head crisp lettuce*
4 *to 6 medium-sized tomatoes, quartered*

Shell the shrimp and remove the veins in backs with a sharp knife. Leave the shrimp whole. Make a sauce by mixing all other ingredients except lettuce and tomatoes. Put the shrimp in the sauce and mix well. Arrange the lettuce and quartered tomatoes on salad plates and distribute the shrimp and sauce over them. Garnish with fresh parsley and mayonnaise, and serve chilled.

Avocado Stuffed with Shrimp

2 *lbs. shrimp, boiled and shelled*
3 *stalks celery*
2 *hard-boiled eggs*
2 *tablespoons parsley*
½ *medium-sized bell pepper*
juice of 1 lemon

¼ *teaspoon sugar*
salt and pepper to taste
mayonnaise to bind all together
black olives
2 *avocados*

The boiling of the shrimp in flavored water as directed on pages 3–4 will make all the difference in the world to this salad's flavor. Chop the ingredients for the filling very fine, except for the shrimp, which should be cut into small segments but not minced or mashed. Mix all together and season. Just before serving time, peel the avocados, cut them in halves, and remove the pits. Then fill the cavity in each avocado half with a mixture of the shrimp and other ingredients. Top the filling with tiny crests of mayonnaise (about ¼ teaspoon) and dot with two quarter-slices of black olives crisscrossed over each other. Serve on lettuce leaves. Serves 4.

Tomato Aspic

Tomato aspic may be served as a first course or as a salad course. It aids digestion, particularly when alcoholic beverages have been served before dinner. This is a comparatively simple salad to make, but it is always impressive. The recipe will serve 4 to 6.

1 No. 2 can tomato juice
1 stalk celery, whole
1 large onion, chopped
½ teaspoon salt
½ teaspoon sugar
¼ teaspoon red or black pepper
2 bay leaves
1 envelope unflavored gelatin

Put the tomato juice in a pot with the celery stalk, onion, all seasonings, and 1 cup water. Boil for 15 minutes. Shut off the fire, let the liquid become lukewarm, and strain it through a colander into another pot. Dissolve the gelatin in 1 cup hot water. Add to the tomato juice. Boil for 5 minutes, stirring. Pour the hot liquid into aspic molds, let cool, then place in the refrigerator to jell. Serve on lettuce leaves when well chilled.

Party Aspic

1 medium-sized can tomatoes
1 small bay leaf
1 can consommé or bouillon
½ clove garlic, put through garlic press
⅓ medium onion, scraped
juice of ¼ lemon
3 very thin slices lemon peel
2 teaspoons red-wine vinegar
1 tablespoon sugar
dash of Tabasco Sauce
1½ tablespoons Worcestershire sauce
salt and pepper to taste
½ box unflavored gelatin
1 cup diced cold cooked vegetables (carrots, string beans, etc.)
¼ cup diced celery
stuffed olives, sliced
2 hard-boiled eggs, sliced

Heat the tomatoes with the bay leaf, consommé, garlic, scraped onion, lemon juice and peel, vinegar, sugar, Tabasco Sauce, and Worcestershire sauce. Add salt and pepper to taste. Soak the gelatin in about ¼ cup cold water until it has softened, and then heat it in a double boiler until melted. Blend with the hot liquids and cool over ice until the mixture begins to thicken. Pour into a mold over cold cooked vegetables, such as carrots and beans, celery, and sliced olives. A layer of olive, carrot, and hard-boiled-egg slices at the bottom of the mold will make an attractive topping for the aspic when it is turned out amid a wreath of crisp lettuce leaves just before serving for buffet luncheon or supper or, sliced, for the salad course of dinner. Serves 8 to 10.

Sweet French Dressing

This is a sweet French dressing with what might be called a mayonnaise base. It makes a bland, delicious dressing for lettuce and tomatoes, green salads, and watercress salad, a dip for boiled crabs, and, when fortified with Burgundy, a wonderful sauce for fresh artichokes. Make up a supply and keep it in your refrigerator, where it will last for weeks.

1 *tablespoon sugar*
dash of black pepper
2 *dashes of paprika*
½ *teaspoon dry mustard*
½ *teaspoon salt*

2 *cloves garlic, halved*
6 *tablespoons olive oil or salad oil*
2 *tablespoons wine vinegar*
1 *tablespoon mayonnaise*

Mix the sugar, pepper, paprika, mustard, and salt in a bowl. Add garlic halves and oil. Rub the garlic well through the ingredients. Add vinegar and stir mayonnaise in well. Let season for 30 minutes, stirring vigorously occasionally. Just before serving on salad, remove the garlic. If you prefer a "dry" French dressing, omit sugar and mayonnaise.

❧ 8 ❧

BISCUITS, BREAD,
AND PIES

Quick Breakfast Rolls

2 *cups flour*
1 *tablespoon sugar*
pinch of salt
1¾ *teaspoons baking powder*

1 *heaping tablespoon lard*
1 *egg, slightly beaten*
¼ *cup milk*
butter

Sift together flour, sugar, salt, and baking powder, then mix the lard lightly into the flour, cutting it in with the side of a spoon and lifting the flour to bring air into it during the cutting and mixing process. When the lard lumps in the flour are the size of large peas and small marbles, stir in the egg, then add enough cold milk (about ¼ cup is ample) to make the mixture the consistency of soft biscuit dough, or to permit the dough to leave the sides of the bowl cleanly. Lift out with a spoon onto a floured board, roll out lightly, cut into disks with a small biscuit cutter, and fold each disk in half over a small piece of refrigerator-hardened butter. Bake immediately in a 400° oven for about 15 minutes. Do not overbake. Serve hot as soon as the rolls turn delicate brown if you want rave notices; the secret of this type of bread is serving it at the strategic moment, right out of the oven. Makes 18 to 20 rolls.

Twisted Rolls

1 *package powdered yeast*
1 *teaspoon sugar*
1 *teaspoon salt*
1½ *tablespoons melted lard*

1 *cup sweet milk*
2 *eggs*
2 *cups flour, sifted twice*
melted butter

Dissolve the yeast in ¼ cup lukewarm water in a mixing bowl. Stir in the sugar, salt, and melted lard; then add the milk and eggs. Stir in the flour and mix well. Cover in a warm room until the dough has risen—about 1 hour. Turn the batter out on a floured board and knead lightly for a minute or so. Roll the dough out about ½ inch thick on the board, cut in strips 2 inches long, and twist. Put in a greased baking pan in a 350° oven. When the rolls are brown, brush them with melted butter.

Coffee Bread

1 *cup flour*
2 *teaspoons baking powder*
¼ *teaspoon salt*
2 *tablespoons granulated sugar*
2 *tablespoons melted fat*
½ *cup milk*

1 *egg, lightly beaten*
⅓ *cup brown sugar*
1 *tablespoon butter*
½ *teaspoon cinnamon*
½ *cup chopped nuts*
¼ *cup raisins*

Sift flour, baking powder, salt, and sugar together. Lightly blend with the melted fat and milk, and fold in the lightly beaten egg. Pour into a shallow greased pan. Mix together the brown sugar, butter, cinnamon, chopped nuts, and raisins, and spread over the dough. Bake 15 minutes in a moderate oven.

Old-Fashioned Hot Biscuits

2 *cups flour (not self-rising flour)*   2 *teaspoons baking powder*
1 *teaspoon salt*   6 *level tablespoons lard (not oil)*
1 *teaspoon sugar*   1 *cup sweet milk*

Sift flour, salt, sugar, and baking powder into a mixing bowl. With the edge of a large kitchen spoon cut the lard into the flour until it is the size of large peas. This should be done lightly with a scooping motion, lifting some of the flour with each stroke rather than mashing the lard into the flour. Then stir in the milk. Cover a board with flour and roll the ball of dough out ½ inch thick. Cut out biscuits with the top of a can or a biscuit cutter, and place in a greased baking pan. Bake 10 to 15 minutes in a 500° oven, until brown. Serve immediately. Keep extra biscuits covered with a napkin. Makes 12 to 15 biscuits.

Hot Muffins

This recipe also will do for waffles or pancakes, if you thin the batter a little with milk or water.

1½ *cups flour*   2 *eggs*
1 *teaspoon sugar*   3 *tablespoons cooking oil or*
1 *teaspoon salt*   *melted fat*
1 *cup cold milk*   2½ *teaspoons baking powder*

Sift the flour into a bowl, add sugar, salt, and milk, stirring until smooth. Beat the eggs and pour them in, stirring well. Add the oil and stir in the baking powder. Grease a muffin pan. Fill the pan ⅔ full with batter. Bake in a 500° oven 15 or 20 minutes. Serves 5 to 6.

Corn Muffins

This recipe makes either cornbread or corn muffins.

1½ *cups cornmeal*   1 *teaspoon sugar*
½ *cup flour*   1 *teaspoon salt*
1 *cup milk*   2 *eggs, beaten*
3 *tablespoons oil or melted lard*   2 *teaspoons baking powder*

Mix the cornmeal and flour with the milk; add oil, sugar, salt, eggs, and stir well. Add the baking powder at the last minute. Grease a baking or muffin pan and half fill the pan with batter. Bake in 375° oven until brown—about ½ hour. Serves 7 to 8.

Corn Cakes

These are not to be confused with ordinary flapjacks. Jesse's corn cakes are crisp, light, and only about ⅛ inch thick. They are a regular breakfast standby at our house, served with honey or maple or corn sirup.

9 *level tablespoons white corn-*   ⅛ *teaspoon salt*
  meal   1 *teaspoon baking powder*
4½ *tablespoons flour*   *oil or fat for frying (Jesse prefers*
½ *teaspoon sugar*   *pure lard)*

Sift the cornmeal into a bowl and add ½ cup hot water, stirring until the mixture creams without lumps. Add flour, sugar, salt, baking powder, and ½ cup cold water and stir until smooth. Cover the bottom of a frying pan with oil or fat, drop tablespoonfuls of batter into the pan, and fry them until crisp and brown, turning each cake once. Serve hot. Makes 12 to 15 cakes, depending on size. Jesse makes small ones about the size of a silver dollar, and larger ones about 3 inches in diameter.

Brandied Peach Fritters

These fritters are not flat like most others I've seen. They're puffy and light, and the jelly gems, nestling on the white sugar frosting, make them a most decorative dish. They're delicious with any sort of roast, steak, chops, or Sunday salad.

½ large can sliced peaches
½ cup brandy or bourbon
  whisky
1¼ cups flour (before sifting)
2½ teaspoons baking powder
4 tablespoons sugar

½ teaspoon salt
3 eggs, well beaten
fat for frying
powdered sugar
apple jelly or mint jelly

Drain the peaches of sirup (saving the sirup) and soak them for at least several hours in the brandy or whisky. When you are ready to make the fritters, sift the flour, baking powder, sugar, and salt into a bowl. Add ½ cup liquid composed of brandy in which the fruit soaked and sirup from the peaches. Fold in the beaten eggs, then add the peaches. Do not have the batter too thin, or the fritters will not hold their shape. Drop in large tablespoonfuls into hot deep fat. Fry to golden brown. Drain on paper, sprinkle with powdered sugar, and just before serving drop a tiny star of clear jelly—apple preferred—atop each fritter. For party occasions apple and mint may be used alternately on fritters for colorful variation.

Bananas may be substituted for the peaches, but they should be soaked in the brandy or whisky for only a few minutes, after being quartered lengthwise and then sliced into small wedges. Mix them with the batter—a bit of milk or water may be added if thinning is needed. Mint or currant jelly or orange marmalade is colorful and delicious atop the banana confections—and they *are* confections in every sense of the word. Mainly because the soaking period is shorter, and also because banana fritters do not necessitate opening a whole can of fruit, I prepare the banana ones more often in our small household. I have many times, in making the fritters for only my husband and myself, halved this recipe, which is Jesse's usual proportion for serving a large family group. In cutting the recipe, use 1 scant cup flour, 2 eggs, and ⅓ cup brandy or whisky. For everything else, cut the proportions given exactly in half.

Piecrust

Jesse doesn't make a lot of very fancy pastries, but pies, those down-to-earth staples of America's favorite dinners, are a feature of his topflight menus. He doesn't make a wide variety of these pastry specials either, or go to a lot of fuss and fanfare in their preparation. But his standbys are as noted as any of his other culinary masterpieces and show the departures from standard recipes that characterize his cooking style.

He uses for his pie-making two types of crust—the pastry shell and the Crumb-Nut Crust—and his favorite and most popular pies are apple, Key lime, and a combination apple-and-peach pie that I have never encountered elsewhere.

Jesse always makes his own piecrust dough because he's done it for so many years that it's practically second nature for him to whip up the pastry in no time flat. In case you want to mix your own, I give his recipes, which are quite simple.

However, I wish to say here that Jesse thinks—and I heartily agree with him—that the prepared piecrust mixes now on the market represent one step in modern cookery that can be safely taken to shorten time and labor, while still maintaining the highest standards. A touch I have learned from Jesse, which greatly enhances the results I get from using pie mixes of almost any brand, is the addition of 1 or 2—sometimes even 3—tablespoons more water than is called for in the directions on the package. Perhaps the makers of piecrust mixes fear that inexperienced cooks will "flood" their dough with too much water and hence prefer people to risk adding too little moisture. Or perhaps most mixes dry out a bit after standing for some weeks on the grocery or kitchen shelf, and can take more moisture than when they left their makers' kitchens. Whatever the reason, Jesse believes most dough made with mixes is too dry when it is prepared strictly according to directions. It handles better, can be rolled thinner without cracking, and is tenderer and crisper when baked, if a bit more water is added. I always add the extra water, very cold, 1 tablespoon at a time, mixing until the dough is not exactly wet, but very damp, does not leave a lot of loose flour on the sides and bottom of the bowl, and does not have a floury look. Jesse handles his pie dough lightly and, as much as possible, with a spoon, and he uses as little flour as possible for rolling. He rolls the dough lightly and quickly with a floured rolling pin, with short, outward, cartwheel strokes. When packaged pie dough is treated in this fashion I would defy any expert to detect it from homemade pastry made from scratch.

But here are Jesse's recipes in case you may want to make your own.

EVERYDAY PIECRUST

This is the crust Jesse uses for meat pies or any non-dessert dish.

2 *cups sifted self-rising flour*   ½ *cup Wesson oil*
⅛ *teaspoon salt*   ¼ *cup cold milk*

Sift flour and salt into a mixing bowl. Pour into a measuring cup (but don't stir together) the oil and milk. Pour into the flour. Stir lightly until mixed. Divide the dough into two parts, one (for bottom crust) slightly larger than the other. Place the larger half between two sheets of waxed paper or on a very lightly floured board. Roll it out *lightly* and place in a pie tin for baking until brown in a 375° to 400° oven, about 20 minutes. Roll out the other half for the top crust. If you're baking a single-crust pie, halve the recipe.

UNIVERSAL PIECRUST

Jesse uses this crust mostly for dessert pies. It may be used for not-so-sweet pie preparations as well, which is the reason he calls it universal. The butter-and-sugar content makes it preferable for party occasions.

2 *tablespoons lard or fat*	½ *teaspoon salt*
4 *tablespoons butter*	½ *teaspoon sugar*
2 *cups sifted flour*	½ *cup fresh milk*

Stir the lard and butter in a bowl until creamy. Sift the flour, salt, and sugar together and add. Mix with milk. If the dough is too thick, add cold water. Spread flour on a board and roll out the dough ¼ inch thick. Place in greased pie pans and indent the edges with a fork. Will make 2 pies.

OLD-FASHIONED PIECRUST

½ *cup lard*	*tiny pinch of salt*
½ *cup butter*	3 *cups sifted flour*

With a knife, blend the lard, butter, and salt into the flour. Moisten with 8 to 10 tablespoons ice water, handling the dough as little as possible. Roll the dough very thin. The recipe may be easily halved for one crust with perfect results.

Crumb-Nut Crust

1 *cup vanilla-wafer crumbs*
¾ *cup grated pecans*

6 *tablespoons butter or oleo-*
   margarine

Mix the crumbs and nuts and blend in the butter or margarine until the mixture can be pressed firmly around the bottom and sides of a 9-inch pie pan. If you go a bit heavy on the butter, you'll find that the crust will hang together well and can be cut and served every bit as satisfactorily as a pastry shell. Bake the shell in a slow oven (300° to 350°) for ½ hour or 40 minutes, until the nuts begin to brown slightly and smell toasty. Remove and let cool. Fill.

Apple Pie

3 *or 4 large apples, peeled and*
  sliced
½ *cup sugar*
½ *cup brown sugar*

nutmeg
cinnamon
1 *scant tablespoon flour*
butter

To the apples add ½ cup sugar (or a bit more, as your taste dictates and according to the sweetness or tartness of the apples), the brown sugar, nutmeg and cinnamon to taste, and the flour. Line a pie pan with pastry and into it pour the mixture. Dot with butter. Cover with a top crust and bake in a fairly hot oven, 450°, about 45 minutes.

A very easy way to be sure that the apples will be cooked as tender as you like them is to stew them with the sugar for a short time before putting them in the crust; let them cool a bit before adding the flour, cinnamon, and nutmeg, and then put them in the crust to bake.

Apple Pie with Canned Apples

I have never yet found the person who guessed that fresh apples were not used for this pie.

1 *large can apples*	*dash of lemon juice*
¼ *cup brown sugar*	*pinch of salt*
½ *cup granulated sugar*	2 *tablespoons flour*
1 *teaspoon cinnamon*	*egg white or canned milk for*
½ *teaspoon nutmeg*	*"polishing" crust*

Jesse blends gently in a mixing bowl all ingredients except the last, and pours the mixture into an unbaked pastry shell. He crisscrosses the top with pastry strips and sprinkles the strips with a mixture of granulated sugar and cinnamon after he has brushed them lightly with egg white or canned milk. He bakes this slowly (350°) for 1 hour or more, until the filling thickens.

Apple-Peach Pie

Jesse uses a larger and deeper pie dish for this pie than for Apple Pie (see page 156), since the filling takes more space. He adds to the apple pie mixture 1 large can peaches. He prefers halved peaches, and slices the fruit himself to make three pieces from each half, as, he explains, this method provides thick sections that don't fall apart in baking. Other ingredients are the same as for Apple Pie except for the addition of 2 extra tablespoons granulated sugar, 1 tablespoon thick sirup from the peaches, and an extra ½ tablespoon flour.

Fleecy Lemon Pie

We usually use Crumb-Nut Crust for our lemon pies, as we do for our lime confection. However, in seasons when pecans are scarce, or when time precludes making the slightly more elaborate crust, we serve this billowy version almost as successfully either on prepared crust or with one of Jesse's recipes for such pastry. Note that there is *no* cornstarch in this recipe.

6 *egg yolks*   3 *egg whites*
1 *scant cup sugar*   *baked pie shell*
juice of 2 *large or* 3 *small lemons*

Beat the egg yolks until creamy and very pale. (You will no doubt think after the first few minutes of beating the yolks that they are light in color. But beat just a bit longer—it's amazing how pale they get before they're ready. I beat mine at least 5 minutes at high speed with my electric mixer.) Slowly sift the sugar into the eggs and continue beating as the sugar is added. Add the lemon juice and beat in, then put the mixture in a double boiler. (I have a very deep double-boiler pot, so that my mixer blades fit into it, and I beat the mixture right in the pot in which I cook it.) Set over boiling water and cook until the mixture holds its shape. Stir constantly to keep from lumping or sticking. Sixteen to 17 minutes should suffice. Remove from boiling water and substitute cold water beneath the mixture. Set aside.

Beat the egg whites until stiff but still moist (do not overbeat) and fold the custard mixture into the whites. Then this whole creamy, frothy creation is poured into the baked pie shell and topped with the meringue described for Key Lime Pie.

Key Lime Pie

Key limes grow semi-wild on the rocky, wind-swept chain of islands extending south and west of the Florida mainland to Key West. The fruit is small, about half the size of a California lemon or Persian lime, and has a distinctive tangy flavor. Natives of the Keys squeeze the juice of the limes and use them to flavor a meringue-covered pie which has become famous not only throughout South Florida but wherever delighted tourists tell of the taste treat of Key Lime Pie.

Most native versions of Key Lime Pie are made with a condensed-milk base. Since the little Key lime doesn't boast much of a rind and carries its own distinctive flavor very strongly in its juice alone, the rind should not be grated as for lemon pies.

Following is the condensed-milk version so well known in Key West, where it is usually served in a baked pastry crust. Jesse rarely serves this version in a pastry crust, however. He much prefers the Crumb-Nut Crust, which adds the flavor of toasted pecans to the delicate lime flavor.

1 *can sweet condensed milk*	¼ *teaspoon cream of tartar*
4 *eggs, separated*	8 *tablespoons sugar, or sugar to*
juice of 4 or 5 key limes	*taste*

Combine the condensed milk, egg yolks, and lime juice, and beat the mixture until it is very thick. Pile into a baked pastry shell or Crumb-Nut Crust. Beat the egg whites until they are bubbly, then add the cream of tartar and continue the beating, adding the sugar gradually. When the mixture will hold firm peaks (the meringue points must not curl over, but stand straight up as the beater is pulled from the bowl), it is ready to be swirled over the pie, and the pie is then ready to be popped into a 400° oven for quick browning. Warning: if you cook this meringue too long it will toughen, so don't try to brown it in too slow an oven. Ten to 15 minutes in a 400° oven will do the trick.

Pecan Pie

A Deep South cookbook would not be complete without a recipe for pecan pie, that intriguing confection that travels all over the map in gift packages sent home by tourists, who may not agree on all Southern dishes, but who generally give overwhelming endorsement to this one.

Here is a recipe that will dispel the mystery of Southern Pecan Pie. The first trial will convince even the rankest amateur that it's no great trouble to turn out one of the South's most favored confections.

4 eggs
1 *heaping cup sugar*
1 *scant tablespoon flour*
¼ *lb. butter, melted*
1 *cup white corn sirup*

1½ *cups pecans, chopped or broken in fairly large pieces*
1 *cup pitted dates, chopped fine*
1 *unbaked pastry shell (Jesse's Old-Fashioned Piecrust is good)*

Beat the eggs well, add sugar and flour, and blend. Stir the melted butter with the sirup, nuts, and dates, and then add to sugar-egg-flour mixture, and blend well. Pour into a deep pie pan lined with an unbaked pastry shell and bake about 40 or 45 minutes at 350°, or until browned.

❦ 9 ❦

DESSERTS
AND BEVERAGES

Watermelon Sherbet

This is one of Jesse's most enticing hot-weather desserts. It may be served in halves of iced cantaloupe or in sherbet glasses with cake or cookies. It is pink in color, with a delicious haunting flavor, unlike any other ice. This recipe will make ½ gallon, or enough to serve 10.

1 20- to 25-lb. watermelon	2 tablespoons fresh lemon juice
about 2½ cups sugar	1 egg white

Cut the watermelon in half, scoop out the meat, and squeeze out the juice through a colander to eliminate seeds. Throw away the pulp. Sweeten the juice with sugar (the amount depends on the sweetness of the melon; be sure to sweeten sufficiently, and remember the juice tastes sweeter before freezing than after it is frozen). Pour in the lemon juice, and freeze the sherbet in ice trays in the freezing unit or compartment of the refrigerator. Stir every 15 minutes to keep the sherbet from getting flaky. When the juice starts to harden, beat up an egg white, mix it in, and stir every 15 minutes until the sherbet stiffens. The sherbet can now be served, and the unconsumed portion can be kept in the freezing compartment for days or even weeks.

Ambrosia

This is one of Jesse's masterpieces, a dish that elicits unfeigned admiration and compliments.

1 *coconut, or 1 can grated coco-*
    nut
6 *firm, ripe bananas*

6 *oranges*
½ *cup granulated sugar*
powdered sugar for top (optional)

Grate the coconut, peel the bananas and oranges, and slice them. Lay slices of bananas and oranges in a layer on the bottom of a dessert bowl, cover with coconut, sprinkle with sugar, and continue to make layers, sprinkling with coconut and sugar, until the slices of fruit are used up. If any coconut is left, add it to the top and sprinkle with sugar. Place in the refrigerator for 1 hour before serving. This will make a delicious, unusual, picturesque dessert. Serves 6 to 7.

Avocado Whip

The avocado—or alligator pear, as it is known in South Florida, where it is grown—is justly renowned as a superlative salad vegetable, but comparatively few people know that it also makes an excellent sweet dessert. This recipe will serve 6.

3 *large or 4 small ripe avocados*
juice of 4 lemons

½ *cup granulated sugar*
whipped cream (optional)

Scoop the meat from the avocados and mash until soft. Add lemon juice and sweeten with granulated sugar. You may vary the amount of sugar to taste. Whip with a wire or rotary beater until smooth. Serve chilled in sherbet glasses, with or without whipped cream on top.

Floating Island

An impressive dessert that tastes as nice as it looks.

4 eggs
1 cup, plus 2 teaspoons, sugar
1½ teaspoons cornstarch

1 qt. milk
2 teaspoons vanilla
nutmeg (optional)

Separate the egg yolks and whites. Add 1 cup sugar and the cornstarch to the yolks, stirring briskly until creamy. Add milk slowly and stir till smooth. Put the mixture in the top of a double boiler over hot water, and stir until thick. Beat the egg whites until stiff, and stir into them the vanilla and 2 teaspoons sugar. Pour the egg whites into the milk mixture, stirring for 5 minutes. Take off the fire and let cool. Dust with nutmeg, if desired. Place in refrigerator. The egg whites will sit on top of the creamy mixture, whence the name "Floating Island." Serves 6 to 7.

Marshmallow Cream

½ pt. heavy cream
½ lb. marshmallows
¼ cup chopped pecans

6 or 8 maraschino cherries
1 teaspoon sugar
½ teaspoon vanilla

In this modern day of the electric refrigerator, electric ice-cream freezer, deep freezers, and drugstores on every corner, quick frozen desserts have all but replaced the simple old-fashioned ones that were so delicious. Here is one that fills me with nostalgia every time Jesse makes it. He cuts the marshmallows in quarters into the cream, and then stirs in the chopped pecans, maraschino cherries, sugar, and vanilla. He chills this in the refrigerator for at least ½ hour and serves it in sherbet glasses, topped with cherries.

Angel Parfait

¾ cup sugar

2 egg whites, beaten to the
   "peak" stage but not dry

1 teaspoon flavoring (vanilla,
   almond, pistachio, or other)

1 pt. whipping cream, whipped
   until stiff

nuts or fruit as desired—pecans
   or almonds, dates or cherries,
   etc.

Combine sugar and ½ cup water, and boil until the sirup spins a thread. Remove from the fire and pour in a thin stream into the beaten egg whites, and continue beating until the mixture is cold. Add the flavoring and fold in the whipped cream. (Do *not* pour the whipped cream into the sirup-egg mixture while the mixture is the least bit hot.) After folding in the cream, pour the whole into a mold (aluminum is your best bet, as most of the so-called "icebox glass" cracks when used for this recipe). Pack in ice and salt for 2 hours, or place in a freezer unit for 1 to 1½ hours, but watch to see that the parfait does not freeze completely. The parfait should be topped with whipped cream or fruit juice. Canned figs, frozen strawberries, fresh sliced and sugared peaches, or other such fruits are delicious for topping. For variety, chopped nuts and dates may be combined with the fruit sirup for serving over the parfait, or they may be added before freezing. Serves 4 to 6.

Nut-Stuffed Baked Apples

8 *large, tart, firm apples*　　　　1¾ *cups sugar*
½ *lemon*　　　　　　　　　　　*cinnamon*
¼ *lb. raisins and dates, mixed*　　*nutmeg*
¾ *lb. almonds or pecans, halved*　1 *teaspoon gelatin*
　and blanched　　　　　　　　*tiny pinch of salt*

Wash, pare, and core the apples (the larger they are, the better). Rub the lemon half well over them. Put the raisins and dates through the food grinder with about one-third of the nuts. Mix well with ¼ cup sugar and a light sprinkling of cinnamon and nutmeg. Set aside. Make a sirup of 1½ cups sugar and 1½ cups water and cook the apples in it until they are soft but not broken. Save the sirup. Place the apples in a deep dish or pan and gently (so as not to break the apples) press into the space where the core was the chopped raisin-date-nut mixture. Put blanched almonds or pecan halves on top. Dredge the nuts and apples with sugar and brown in the oven. Soak the gelatin in 1 tablespoon water. When the apples have browned, remove from the oven and place in a serving dish. Heat the sirup and add slowly to the gelatin. Pour the mixture over the apples. Serve cold, either plain or with whipped cream or ice cream. A nice variation is the addition to the boiling sirup of red coloring that will give the apples a deep, ruby tint. However, you will find that the plain, rich, glossy brown color of the natural baked apple is very attractive as is.

Guava Duff

This is a famed Key West dessert introduced into our cookery via my husband's mother's kitchen. It is a tart, tasty, pudding-type confection, classically topped with hard sauce well spiked with Cuban rum. The trick nowadays is to get the fresh guavas that grow plentifully in South Florida; no other fruit, it seems to me, makes duff the way guavas do, though the Key Westers make this same kind of dessert with dates, raisins, and coconuts.

2 *cups guava pulp*	4 *teaspoons baking powder*
1 *generous cup sugar*	½ *teaspoon salt*
⅛ *lb. butter*	3 *cups flour*
3 *eggs, well beaten*	

The guava pulp is prepared by simmering thinly sliced guavas in about ½ cup water for a few minutes, until soft.

Cream the sugar and butter and add the beaten eggs. Add the guava pulp and beat until smooth. Sift the baking powder, salt, and flour into the mixture very slowly, beating until the mixture is smooth and stiff. Some Key Westers line a can with greased paper, pour the guava mixture into the can, and stand the can in a pot with boiling water a little more than halfway up the side of the can. They then steam the duff for about 2 hours. My mother-in-law cooks it just as successfully in an ordinary double boiler, but this method takes 3 to 4 hours. The mixture comes from the can or pot in one piece, is chilled, and then sliced and served with hard sauce.

HARD SAUCE

1 *cup powdered sugar (or granu- lated sugar)*	½ *cup butter*
	2 *oz. rum or brandy*

Beat the sugar and butter together until light in color, creamy, and extremely fluffy. Add the rum or brandy and continue beating until thoroughly blended. Granulated sugar may be used in this recipe if powdered sugar is not available—my mother and father, as a matter of fact, preferred hard sauce made with granulated sugar. (Slightly more granulated sugar may have to be used to get the sauce to the proper stiffness.) Chill and serve.

Quick Ladyfinger Shortcake

A quaint old-fashioned favorite of my mother, for luncheons or afternoon teas, was a ladyfinger shortcake. This recipe will provide enough to fill a large dessert or party platter.

36 *ladyfingers*
1 *large or 2 small cans crushed pineapple*

3 *or 4 teaspoons rum*
1 *small jar maraschino cherries*
½ *pt. whipped cream*

Separate the ladyfinger halves. Into the dish in which the shortcake will be served, place a layer of the ladyfinger halves, flat side up. Spread over these a layer of pineapple, then place a layer of the halves, flat side down. Add another layer of pineapple and another layer of cake halves, and so on until all are used up. Combine the rum and the juice from the small bottle of maraschino cherries and pour over all. Place in the refrigerator to marinate and chill. Just before serving, cut the cherries in halves or quarters, combine with whipped cream, and top the shortcake with the mixture.

Fresh or frozen strawberries may be substituted for the pineapple, and small bits of pineapple may be used in the cream topping; or strawberries may be substituted for the cherries. Sliced canned peaches, with either cherries or strawberries in the cream, are delicious too. And variations substituting ice cream (vanilla, cherry, strawberry, peach, or pistachio) for the whipped cream were put to the test—successfully, as always— in the early years when many of Jesse's menus centered on Mother's traditional summertime lawn parties or salon teas. Serves 4 to 6.

Pecan Strips

A typically Deep South culinary gem was given to me by Kathleen Danielson, of Pass Christian, Mississippi, just across the Bay of St. Louis from our own home town. Kathleen, a gifted horticulturalist who developed her garden-club hobby into a profitable nursery business that is one of the few of its size and distinction owned and operated by a woman, is just as good a mother and cook as she is a floral expert. While she has become one of the country's outstanding collectors of and experts on the Deep South's beautiful hibiscus, she has also had time to develop several prize recipes. Following is the detailed formula for Pecan Strips, which Jesse has treasured as much as I have, just as she wrote it for us and as it still appears on the yellowing paper used through the years.

1 *cup sifted flour*	1 *teaspoon vanilla*
½ *cup butter*	1 *cup pecans (broken)*
2 *eggs*	½ *cup coconut (the dry kind)*
1½ *cups brown sugar*	*powdered sugar*
½ *teaspoon salt*	*lemon juice*
½ *teaspoon baking powder*	*salt*
2 *tablespoons flour*	

"Cream together until it is a paste (at first it looks like coarse meal, but it *does* turn into a paste) the 1 cup of flour and butter. Spread in a pan 9″ x 12″ and bake 12 minutes at 350°. Sounds silly, doesn't it?

"While it bakes, beat together the eggs, brown sugar, salt, baking powder, 2 tablespoons flour, vanilla, pecans, and coconut. Pour this mixture over the butter-flour mixture that has baked 12 minutes. Bake this 25 or 30 minutes at 325° or 350°. Cool in pan and then ice with powdered sugar creamed with lemon juice and a pinch of salt. Cut in strips.

"It sounds a little difficult, I know, but it really isn't at all, and

I absolutely guarantee it to bring compliments thick and fast. The icing should be very thin. I didn't measure the powdered sugar, but it takes less than a cup. Leave cake in the pan to ice and cut in strips, because the stuff on the bottom will fall off if it is handled too much. The strips will lift out nicely when cooled."

Layer Cake

This is a standard cake with which almost any kind of jelly or fruit can be served.

¼ *lb. butter*	2½ *teaspoons baking powder*
½ *cup sugar*	¼ *teaspoon salt*
2 *eggs, separated*	1 *cup milk*
2 *cups flour*	1 *teaspoon vanilla*

Cream the butter, add the sugar, and beat until fluffy. Beat the egg yolks and add. Sift together the flour, baking powder, and salt, and add. Add the milk. Beat the egg whites until stiff, and fold them in. Add vanilla. Grease two pie pans with butter. Pour in the batter and bake in a 350° oven 20 minutes. Remove from pans and cool. Put apple jelly—or any other fruit jelly—between layers and serve.

Very Best Fruit Cake

This recipe makes 10 pounds. You may cut it in half if you wish, but don't say I didn't warn you to go ahead and make the 10 pounds while the making is good. The difference in cost is not prohibitive, and small indeed when you see how many Christmas gifts can come out of it. For, what with all the attractive wrappings available at the dime store, you won't need special boxes or tins, and your friends will bless you for a 1- or 2-pound morsel of Jesse's fruit cake. Time and energy involved are just about the same for the whole amount—and this is a literal fact, except perhaps for shelling ½ pound more almonds and pecans and pitting ½ pound more dates. So think twice before you decide to whack Jesse's priceless formula in two!

1 *lb. candied cherries*
1 *lb. candied pineapple*
1 *lb. raisins*
1 *lb. dates*
1 *lb. lemon peel*
1 *lb. orange peel*
½ *lb. citron*
½ *lb. pecans*
½ *lb. almonds*
1½ *cups rum*
4 *cups flour*
1 *cup shortening*

1 *cup sugar*
1 *cup honey*
10 *eggs, well beaten*
2 *scant teaspoons salt*
2 *teaspoons baking powder*
2 *teaspoons allspice*
1 *teaspoon nutmeg*
1 *teaspoon powdered cloves*
12 *tablespoons fruit juice (grape, grapefruit, and orange juice mixed, or mostly orange juice —I prefer the latter)*

Prepare the fruit and peel it, shell the nuts, and put all through the food chopper. Stir the rum in well and let stand in a closed vessel overnight. Next morning, dredge the fruit in ½ cup flour. Cream the shortening with the sugar and add the honey. Stir in the beaten eggs and beat till smooth. Sift the remaining flour with the dry ingredients and add. Add the fruit juices and blend thoroughly. Pour the batter over the floured fruit and mix until all fruit is well covered with batter. Line greased baking pans with *three layers* of waxed paper, allowing ½ inch of paper to extend above all sides of the pans. Pour the batter into the pans. Do *not* flatten it. Put into the oven with the cake a pan containing 2 cups water, and replenish the water while baking. This moisture gives a high gloss and nice texture to the cake. Bake 4 hours at 250°.

Jesse makes the cake and stores it in tins, well ahead of Christmas. He "cures" it by pouring, from time to time, ½ jigger, or more, of rum, over the top of the cake. Treated thus, it is a fit companion, in fact an appropriate partner, for the brandied cherries and mint cordial (see page 176) that add so much to Yuletide or Carnival conviviality in the Southland's merriest homes.

Blond Pecan Fudge

Jesse never was much on making candy, but his one recipe for a smooth caramel or custard fudge is the simplest and non-failingest (to coin a welcome kitchen term) homemade candy I have ever encountered—and I tried pretty nearly all the standard recipes during the prolonged candy-making days of my childhood, high school, and college years, and then as a cooking editor who took her job practically and seriously.

This candy is unique, with a creamy, rich, fudgelike, custard-caramel consistency and a flavor that can hardly be described but which seems to blend better with pecans and other nuts than any other I have ever tried.

2 *cups sugar*	1 *cup chopped nut meats, pref-*
1 *small can evaporated milk*	*erably pecans or Brazil nuts*
1 *egg*	1 *teaspoon vanilla extract*
butter the size of an egg	*butter for greasing platter*

Place the first four ingredients in a medium-sized deep pot (either aluminum or granite will do). Stir all together (it is not necessary or even desirable to beat the mixture).

Set the pot on a medium flame and stir continually. If dark flecks appear in the custard-like mixture as it boils, it is a sign that the fire is too high; the egg and butter brown very easily. Simply remove the pot for a few minutes while you scrape the bottom to prevent further sticking; then replace it on the fire and continue stirring. If the heat cannot be lowered sufficiently, use an asbestos pad. Don't be too alarmed at the brown flecks, since they will "beat out" with constant stirring, and the mixture will begin to darken as the candy cooks along, so that the dark spots will finally disappear. Just take care that the bottom is cleared, so that no scorching occurs.

After about 20 minutes of brisk boiling, the candy's foamy appearance will change; the bubbles will get bigger and more widely separated. The candy will begin to be very noisy as the big bubbles pop boisterously. At this point you will know that the candy is nearly done. Tip the pot toward you. When the mixture begins to leave the bottom of the pan completely it is almost ready to remove from the fire, but continue cooking until when a drop is dropped on a plate or slab it may be picked up without sticking to the surface or feeling thin and gooey when pressed between the fingers.

As the candy gets really done the oil of the butter seems to cover it and it acquires a fudgelike consistency when you mash it on the slab with a finger. A sugary dryness also begins to appear on the sides of the pot. Do not allow the candy to overcook. If you are in doubt, remove it for a few minutes from the fire and beat it a bit to cool it slightly—it doesn't hurt to put it back on the flame if it's not quite ready.

After removing from the stove, add the chopped nut meats and vanilla extract, then beat briskly to blend in nuts and flavoring. (Prolonged beating is entirely unnecessary.) Pour onto a greased plate or slab. Cut into squares when the candy hardens, before it gets too cool. This candy stays soft and fresh, keeps its creamy flavor, dries out more slowly, than any other fudge I have ever encountered. This recipe yields approximately 1 pound. It may be doubled with perfect results.

Christmas Eggnog

Use the Floating Island recipe (page 163) but omit the vanilla and stir in ½ teaspoon grated nutmeg. Add ½ pint good rum or whisky just before serving. Serve hot or cold.

Coffee Brûlot

Brew a pot of strong coffee—6 to 8 cups. Place the coffee in a *brûlot* pot or deep silver dish. Break 3 sticks of cinnamon into the coffee and add 1 teaspoon whole cloves, 1 teaspoon allspice, and 3 lumps of sugar. Pour in 2 tablespoons rum or 2 tablespoons good whisky. Light with a match and stir flames and coffee with a long spoon. When the flames die out, serve the coffee in demitasse cups or scooped-out orange halves.

Hot Rum and Tea
with Apple and Lemon

A charming variation on the conventional hot tea served for luncheons or afternoon teas is one that my mother learned first hand from a band of Spanish gypsies. She and I once visited a wandering tribe camped near Bay St. Louis, and Mother spied a family gathered around a gleaming brass samovar having afternoon refreshment.

The gypsies served their tea piping hot in tall glasses, which we found rather difficult to hold but which they seemed not to mind at all. But the novelty of their tea-drinking, and the one Mother adopted on the spot, was their custom of pouring the steaming hot tea over slices of unpeeled apple and lemon. I shall never forget the delicious aroma thus created, as the fragrances of tea, apple, and lemon combined and filled the gypsy tent under the pine trees on that crisp autumn afternoon. Hot tea without a slice of apple will never taste quite the same to me— nor to anyone else who has once tried this gypsy blend. Besides, as Mother quickly discovered, the bright slices of apple and lemon, with clove-starred centers, always provide a picturesque and colorful addition to any tea table. Jesse advises that the apple be fresh-cut as needed throughout the afternoon, so that it doesn't wilt or discolor because of too long exposure to air.

A delightful variation on the gypsy tea itself is one I evolved from boiling 4 or 5 apples and the juice and skins from 2 or 3 lemons in about 1 quart well-sweetened water. Boil covered until the apples are tender (they will turn a bit dark, but that doesn't matter). Just before serving, dip 4 or 5 teaballs into the pot for 4 or 5 minutes, until the brew is well colored and flavored. Grate nutmeg liberally over the top, pour over the apple slices in cups, and spike well with dark rum. This convivial potion is guaranteed to give a party twice the sparkle on half the rum. It is especially good on a cold winter's night and excellent for Thanksgiving, Christmas, or New Year's parties.

Brandied Cherries and Mint Cordial

For after-the-ball Carnival supper parties or receptions, brandied cherries and mint cordial are traditional—you may serve them separately, or, as most families in the Mardi Gras city do, combine them. Both concoctions are extremely simple to prepare but are always begun weeks, and sometimes even months, ahead of time. Jesse's methods for these convivial additions to any Christmas, New Year's, or Easter party follow.

BRANDIED CHERRIES

Invest in 1 gallon high-quality, plump maraschino cherries in heavy sirup, open the jar, pour off all but about one-third, or slightly less, of the sugar-water, and refill the jug with brandy or high-grade 90-to-100-proof whisky. Then store the jug carefully in a secret place and forget about the whole thing until the Great Day or Night. Then bring out the merry little red fireballs to light up even the dullest party. Serve them in a crimson mound on a cut-glass platter, with a frosty sprinkling of powdered sugar dusted on for brilliance.

The whisky or brandy left after removal of the cherries *can* be drunk as a cordial, though it will be too sweet for most tastes. Or you can use it as a base for old-fashioneds.

MINT CORDIAL

For mint cordial obtain tender sprouts of fresh, crisp, young mint kissed only by the full-blown spring or early summer suns. A good handful of these mint sprigs—stems, leaves, and all—should be carefully washed. Shake the washed sprigs clear of water; lay them tenderly in a deep vessel (we have found an old-fashioned glass candy jar with frosted top most suitable for this purpose). Cover with good whisky or brandy (we like bourbon best), close the jar tightly, and let stand 24 hours. Then strain through a coarse cloth, and to every quart of the liquor add 1 pint sugar. Stir well until all is dissolved, and then bottle.

Yes, the brandied or "whisky-ed" cherries may be munched alone, or—you guessed it!—they may be dropped, with devastating results, into the mint cordial. The cordial may be served at room temperature, but will be superbly enhanced if it is poured over crushed ice.

INDEX

179